Praise for

UNLIKELY RADICALS

"This short book gives many gifts: it's the thrilling story of a community fighting off an environmental assault; a series of delightful sketches of ordinary people who accomplish extraordinary things; a cautionary tale of democratic institutions being corrupted by money and shady politics; and an introduction to Charlie's funny, generous, and tough-minded charm. Most importantly, it is a guide book for anyone who is called upon to stand up for what they believe in."

— GORD PERKS, environmental activist, teacher, writer,
    and Toronto city councillor

"I have practiced and taught community organizing all my life and I love this book. Angus—a key insider—tells the story with passion and respect. The detailed account and strategic analysis offered in *Unlikely Radicals* makes the book essential reading for anyone facing a similar struggle."

— JOAN KUYEK, author, *Community Organizing: A Holistic Approach*

Unlikely Radicals

The Story of the
Adams Mine Dump War

CHARLIE ANGUS

Between the Lines
Toronto

Unlikely Radicals: The Story of the Adams Mine Dump War
© 2013 Charlie Angus

First published in 2013 by
Between the Lines
401 Richmond Street West, Studio 277
Toronto, Ontario M5V 3A8
Canada
1-800-718-7201
www.btlbooks.com

Library and Archives Canada Cataloguing in Publication

Angus, Charlie, 1962 –

Unlikely radicals : the story of the Adams Mine dump war / Charlie Angus.
Includes bibliographical references and index.
Issued also in electronic format.

ISBN 978-1-77113-040-0

1. Environmental protection—Citizen participation.   2. Sanitary landfills—Ontario—Boston (Township)—Public opinion.   3. Waste disposal sites—Ontario—Boston (Township)—Environmental aspects.   4. Green movement—Ontario—Boston (Township).   5. Human ecology—Political aspects.   6. Local government and environmental policy—Ontario.   7. Adams Mine (Ont.)—Environmental conditions.   8. Boston (Ont. : Township):—Environmental conditions.   I. Title.

TD171.7.A55   2013   363.7'0525   C2012-907738-0

Cover and text design by Gordon Robertson
Front cover photo by Charlie Angus. For details, see page 26.

Printed in Canada

RECYCLED
Paper made from
recycled material
FSC® C103567

Between the Lines gratefully acknowledges assistance for its publishing activities from the Canada Council for the Arts, the Ontario Arts Council, the Government of Ontario through the Ontario Book Publishers Tax Credit program and through the Ontario Book Initiative, and the Government of Canada through the Canada Book Fund.

Canada Council
for the Arts

Conseil des Arts
du Canada

ONTARIO ARTS COUNCIL
CONSEIL DES ARTS DE L'ONTARIO
50 YEARS OF ONTARIO GOVERNMENT SUPPORT OF THE ARTS
50 ANS DE SOUTIEN DU GOUVERNEMENT DE L'ONTARIO AUX ARTS

To my dear friend and mentor Jack Layton.
He never shied away from a good fight.

Contents

Acknowledgements

This book would not have been possible without the meticulous recordkeeping of Kathy Martin, Joe Muething, Terry Graves, and Barb Biederman-Bukowski. Thanks as well to advice from John Vanthof, Pierre Belanger, Franz Hartmann, Kathy Hakola, and Stan Gorzalczynski. Thanks to *The Temiskaming Speaker* for their photographic and written archives. Thanks to the team at Between the Lines for their precision in reviewing the manuscript.

A special acknowledgement to my wife, Brit Griffin, who should have written this book. I had asked her to write the book with me but she said she didn't want to live through the Adams Mine years a second time. As a result, she was forced to live through them again and again as I researched, edited, and re-edited the text. Special thanks to Brit and my three daughters, Mariah, Siobhan, and Lola, for their patience and love.

The Adams Mine was just another hole until Metro Toronto nearly fell in it.

— *The Toronto Star*, February 6, 1996

This is not a local issue. This is not a regional issue or even a national issue; your fight is of international importance. What you do to stop the importing and burning of toxic waste from the U.S. and Mexico must be known by people all across the continent.

— DR. PAUL CONNETT, April 28, 2002

Virtually all successful garbage battles are won primarily through shrewd, tenacious political action and not through litigation or regulatory proceedings.

— NYPIRG, "No Time to Waste," 1989

The Watershed

I AM OFTEN ASKED THE QUESTION "What got you into politics?" I always think back to a cold October night in 2000, when I stood on a makeshift barricade on the Adams Mine Road. Across the road, police were lining up for mass arrests. But the people who were holding the line weren't radicals, they were my neighbours—many of them senior citizens and farmers. Up until that moment, I had never considered a life in politics. I believed that organized politics was the domain of stuffy old men. I was the guitar player in the alt-country band Grievous Angels. I worked as a local freelance journalist and didn't even consider myself an environmentalist. But as I stood on that barricade, I realized that the people who should have been there to protect the public interest had sold us out.

The proposal to dump millions of tonnes of waste into the fractured pits of the Adams Mine was bitterly opposed by people in my region. The plan was full of risk. Throughout the planning process, local citizens attempted to have their concerns addressed. They participated in the public hearings. They trusted that officials would do the right thing. But they soon learned otherwise. At every step of the way, the men in the fat ties and the women in grey pantsuits flagged ahead a project that should have been rejected out of hand.

As a result, small-town Northern Ontario was forced to take the extraordinary step of putting up barricades to protect their right to be heard.

This act of radical resistance would never have been necessary if public officials had done their job. This realization moved me from observer to activist, to organizer, and eventually to a leader in the fight.

All landfill proposals generate controversy, but the Adams Mine garbage proposal brought Northern Ontario to the brink of conflict. A rural region of 35,000 fought five separate campaigns against the Adams Mine proposal. Each campaign was an increasingly high-stakes affair that included mass demonstrations, blockades, and non-violent resistance.

In pushing the project forward, the provincial government of Mike Harris dismantled long-standing environmental protection measures in the Province of Ontario and opened the door to international PCB import schemes from Japan, the United States, and Mexico. The region of Timiskaming (locally also spelled Temiskaming) became ground zero for a waste battle that was international in scope. The fight against these projects started in small northern Legion halls and ended at an international NAFTA tribunal.

Gordon McGuinty launched this war. In his self-published memoir, *Trashed*, this former ski bum from North Bay suggests that the people who stood on that barricade were part of a "sophisticated form of political terrorism" bankrolled by a secret slush fund of $800,000 in "foreign" money.[1] There was no secret bank account, and the people who stood in his path were the furthest thing from terrorists. What made them radicals was their determination to have a say in whether or not the watershed of their region would be used as part of a massive experiment in waste dumping.

This is the story of how a dump fight morphed into a two-decade campaign of creative and determined civil resistance. Along the way, we trashed Toronto's Olympic bid in Switzerland, organized road blockades, and hired private detectives to track down backroom investors. Numerous political careers were burned up in this fight.

But the real success of the campaign was the effort to build bridges between groups that had previously been divided. And thus we came together—First Nations people and farmers, environmentalists and miners, urban and rural folks, anglophones and francophones. In the crucible of a dump war, community was built and community won out. For me, the lessons learned in this fight have served as a roadmap for my life in federal politics. I learned that the democratic rights of citizens must be rooted in access to fair public process backed up by an uncompromised public service.

I decided to write the history of the Adams Mine war because I believe that accountable public process is under threat like never before. Under the Conservative government of Stephen Harper, basic standards for economic accountability are being stripped through omnibus legislation. Credible and independent bodies like Rights and Democracy or the National Round Table on the Environment and the Economy have been shut down because they challenged the Conservative agenda. The ability of citizens' groups and First Nations to participate in the review of controversial environmental projects has been limited. The legitimate rights of citizens to speak up against the Enbridge pipeline has been undermined with jingoistic accusations against "extremists" and "agitators."

The implications of the Harper government's attack on democratic accountability are of a much greater scale than anything attempted during the Adams Mine war. And yet, there are lessons that can be learned. The Adams Mine project was driven by big money, backroom lobbyists, and a militant right-wing government. But despite holding all the cards, they still lost. They were beaten by an army of volunteers who out-researched, out-organized, and out-strategized them. This book tells the story of how a bunch of farmers, retirees, and First Nations people stood up to the Man and kicked his ass. For this reason alone, it is a story worth telling.

1

The Set-up
1989–1991

Nobody is interested in shoving garbage down anybody's throat.
This is the first step—it's only a small step along the way.
None of this constitutes approval of the deal.
— GORDON McGUINTY, August 1990

Trying to stop [this process] once it's begun
will be like trying to stop a monster.
— Kirkland Lake miner MAURICE LABINE to Gordon McGuinty, 1989

The Site

THE FIRST TIME Gordon McGuinty peered over the rim of South Pit at the Adams Mine, the sight took his breath away. It was 1989 and he had come north to check out this soon-to-be-dead iron ore mine. He hoped that getting access to the huge pits near Kirkland Lake would give him the inside track on the biggest dump contract in the country.

I also came north in 1989, but my search was for something much more modest—I wanted to find a place to raise my young family. My wife,

Brit Griffin, and I had fallen in love with the patch quilt beauty of the Timiskaming region in Northern Ontario. Running along the Quebec border, Timiskaming reflects a fascinating mix of influences; rural and blue-collar communities are set amidst a contrasting landscape of wild wilderness and farm fields.

My wife and I settled in Cobalt in the southern part of the region. This ragged, old silver mining town once boasted two professional hockey teams, numerous live theatres, and an extensive streetcar system. But that was long ago. Like the rest of the region, Cobalt felt like a place that was being slowly swallowed up by geography and history.

The Adams Mine sat on a ridge at the upper edge of the Timiskaming region. South Pit was the deepest of five artificial canyons that had been mined on the eight-thousand-acre site between 1964 and 1990. In addition to South Pit, the other main pits were Central and Peria, along with two smaller pits known as Roche and North. Perhaps the only thing Gordon McGuinty and I will ever agree on is our shared sense of wonder at looking at South Pit for the first time. He describes the breath-taking view in his memoir *Trashed*. I had the same sensation when I first laid eyes on the pit in the late 1990s. The pit walls dropped six hundred feet to a body of beautiful, clear water. A few birds skimmed along the calm surface. The pit stretched nearly two thousand feet across. It was like looking down from the height of a sixty-storey skyscraper.

But when McGuinty first looked over this immense canyon, there was no body of water. In 1989, South Pit was still a working mine. It was loud, dusty, and industrial. Giant scoop shovels clawed out blasted iron ore that was then shovelled into eighty-five-tonne Euclid ore trucks. The trucks would lumber from the pit floor to surface along a hundred-foot-wide haulage roadway that was built on a slow incline supported by huge rock benches fifty and seventy-five feet in height. From the top of the pit, the benches looked like steps on a long, circular staircase.

The bench walls were a source of constant concern for mine engineers. Engineering reports paid close attention to the deep set of fractures

Adams Mine South Pit. PHOTO: Lise Beaudry, courtesy of Adams Mine Coalition

that cut across the roadway. Years of blasting had only made the situation worse. By the late 1980s, the fractures had worked their way down the length of the ramp. Constant maintenance, in the form of huge steel pins and grouting, were needed to prevent the roadbed from sliding into the pit below.[1]

If McGuinty had undertaken his tour of South Pit with the provincial geologist for the region, Larry Jensen, he would have learned of Dr. Jensen's field studies on the movement of water through the pits. Jensen was the foremost geological expert in the province on the Adams Mine. At South Pit he noted serious problems with water flow in the pit: "It is a 200 metre deep hole in very highly fractured rock. High water pressures occur in fractures in the rocks which form the steep walls of the pit. Many cave-ins and collapses of the walls occurred during the operation of the pit."[2]

Jensen had mapped the flow of water in the adjacent Central Pit. He noted that once Central Pit had been mined out in the 1980s and the pumps turned off, groundwater began flowing into the cavern. But when it reached a certain point, the water levelled off. Groundwater flowed in through the fractures in the north rock wall and "out the other side toward the lower elevated land to the south. . . . To this day, that pit is still not filled with water and no surface water runs from it no matter how much it rains or snows from year to year."[3]

The north-south flow of groundwater through South and Central pits followed the general flow of a much larger and relatively unde-fined underwater aquifer. The mine was just south of a continental geo-graphical tipping point known as the Arctic watershed. At the watershed, the long, steady climb of the armadillo-like Canadian Shield levels off. Waters to the north of this tipping point flow towards the Arctic Ocean, while the waters to the south flow towards the St. Lawrence.

In the coming years, the flow of water would become the key issue for opposition to the Adams Mine. The water-filled canyons of the Adams Mine overlook the rich wheat and canola farm fields of the Little Clay Belt region. Hundreds of farm families, Franco-Ontarian and anglophone, depended on the flow of clean water that passed southerly through the underground fractures of the Shield.

You have to admire McGuinty's chutzpah as he pondered pitching South Pit as a destination for Toronto waste. By the mid-1980s the landfill busi-ness in North America had fallen under the control of three international giants—BFI (Browning-Ferris Industries), WMI (Waste Management, Inc.), and Laidlaw Inc. McGuinty had never worked for a waste operator. He had no engineering degree and no capital. But he had spent the previous fourteen years as the salesperson for a number of failed dump ventures.

McGuinty got his start in the business in 1975 when his friend Maurice Lamarche invited him to help promote the abandoned Hilton mine pit near Shawville, Quebec, as a potential site for Ottawa's garbage. McGuinty went door to door selling the project. He pressured reluctant politicians to sign on to the Hilton Mine dump proposal. In a sales pitch much like McGuinty would later use for the Adams Mine, McGuinty and Lamarche told sceptical residents that the abandoned mine was an ideal site because the rock was "impervious" to leakage. They promised to set up an elaborate (but unproven) system to pump and treat leachate from a landfill they promised was "the best site in North America."[4] Despite his best promotional efforts, the town eventually sent him packing.

Undeterred, he took this roughhouse initiation as a training ground for future fights. He tried pitching landfill proposals in North Bay, Sault Ste. Marie, Sturgeon Falls, and Nipissing First Nation. In 1988, he travelled to the Adirondack Mountains in New York hoping to talk the owner of the closed Benson Iron Ore Mine into letting him turn it into a garbage dump. The owner refused, saying he didn't want to be seen as a bad local citizen by turning the property over to dump promoters.[5]

After fourteen years of trying, McGuinty didn't have much to show for his efforts. But he had learned lessons from each one of these defeats. "I was getting smarter," McGuinty writes in his memoir. "While environmental issues remained paramount, I had now learned it takes political will to find disposal solutions. I learned that in finding waste management solutions, political considerations will often trump common sense . . . environmentally superior solutions are often by-passed."[6]

There was nothing about the badly fractured pits of the Adams Mine that suggested it was an "environmentally superior" location. In fact, the terrain was the diametric opposite of what was considered appropriate for a modern urban landfill.

In the postwar era, concerns about groundwater contamination had pushed municipalities towards standardizing dump site construction based on an emerging science of landfills. The fundamental principle was to ensure that leachate (garbage ooze) could be contained and prevented from making contact with underlying groundwater aquifers. The typical landfill was constructed as a series of long, shallow cells, each separated from the other by layers of protective plastic and clay liners. The cells were built atop a natural base of thick clay separating the waste from the underlying water table.

Heather Rogers describes a typical landfill liner in her book *Gone Tomorrow: The Hidden Life of Garbage*:

Liners . . . generally look like this: several feet of earth are hard packed; then a half inch layer of bentonite clay padding ("Claymax") is laid down. Next comes 60 mm-gauge black plastic sheeting made of high-density polyethylene (HDPE; a thicker version of the material used for milk and detergent jugs); an inch thick plastic drainage mesh is then installed; on top of that goes another layer of bentonite padding and 60 mm HDPE; then a half inch thick synthetic felt fabric layer gets laid down to protect the layers underneath. Topping it all off is eighteen inches of gravel to facilitate drainage.7

There was no clay base at the South Pit. There was no possibility of lining the fractured walls with bentonite or polyethylene. Rather than a series of shallow cells, it was a very deep hole plunging hundreds of feet straight through a fractured water table. Nothing like this had been tried before.

But McGuinty didn't need to worry himself about the technical problems at this stage. In the landfill business, it was the job of the hired consultants to figure out how the problems of a site could be turned to an advantage. Canada's biggest city was desperate to find a massive hole. Gordon McGuinty knew that if he had access to the Adams Mine, he'd be in the driver's seat of a very lucrative garbage venture.

The Crisis

As Gordon McGuinty stared into the depths of South Pit, officials at Toronto City Hall were peering into an abyss of their own. The Keele Valley landfill had been built to solve the city's garbage problem for a generation, but it was filling up quicker than anyone had anticipated. The city's phenomenal growth in population had resulted in an equally phenomenal growth in garbage. *Toronto Star* columnist Royson James pegged the annual garbage production at about 3.2 million tonnes a year—"enough to fill 800,000 garbage trucks that would stretch bumper to bumper from Toronto to Vancouver."[8]

It was proving problematic to find a new site. The city was landlocked by municipalities that were also growing at staggering rates. The surrounding regions of Peel, Durham, and York were struggling with their own waste management problems. The last thing they wanted to do was to provide valuable real estate for their bigger neighbour to dump diapers and empty pop bottles.

When the process of getting Keele Valley into operation started back in 1967, the Maple Pits (as they were known) were situated in the tiny rural town of Maple just north of the city. By the time Toronto began shipping waste to the site in the mid-1980s, Maple had been swallowed up into an ever-growing suburban belt. The twenty-million-tonne landfill was now smack dab in the middle of suburbia, and its neighbours were hostile to any efforts to expand the operation. As more and more garbage trucks headed north to Keele Valley, Toronto faced the prospect of having the landfill filled in before it managed to locate another elusive dump location.

This isn't to say the city hadn't tried hard. The problem was that nobody wanted to become Toronto's dumping ground. At the time, Toronto was made up of the downtown city and five suburban boroughs. Garbage was handled by the overall governing body of Metro Toronto. Metro's planners found themselves fighting numerous battles in townships across southern Ontario as they searched out alternative possibilities.

In the early 1970s, Metro's plan to ship 400,000 tonnes a year to Hope Township by train was stopped by local opposition. Attempts by Toronto and neighbouring suburban municipalities to set up garbage incinerators or dumps in other Southern Ontario communities were greeted by wave after wave of backlash. Numerous local groups were formed in communities like Warwick, Orillia, Petrolia, and Harwich Township.

They used names like PAGE (Petrolians Against Garbage Export), HOPE (Haldimand Organization for a Pure Environment), TNT (Take No Trash), and We Care (a Harwich Township citizens' group).

Across rural Southern Ontario, local politicians learned that there was no political future in being on the wrong side of a garbage import fight. Many of the first not-in-my-back-yard politicians were Tories. Southern Ontario backbenchers understood that standing up to big, bad Toronto made for good local politics. The Progressive Conservative government of Bill Davis took a hard line with Metro Toronto—look after your own waste. As Harold Crooks explains in *Giants of Garbage*, the political implications were clear: "Conservatives would not allow Metro to dump its trash in constituencies that faithfully re-elected their members to Queen's Park."[9]

Toronto waste planners looked internally to working-class River-dale as a possible site for incineration. The grassroots pushback against burning garbage along the waterfront launched a generation of Toronto activist politicians, including Marilyn Churley, Sandra Bussin, and Jack Layton. The Riverdale resistance in the 1980s forced City Hall to recon-sider the need for more-distant and less-politically-organized regions. Even though the Toronto waste contract was still in municipal hands, waste planners were following the same pattern that was emerging in the United States. Large U.S. cities had begun exporting their waste to rural or underprivileged jurisdictions. This move was hastened by the priva-tization of the garbage industry. Corporate behemoths like BFI and WMI dominated the North American garbage industry through their devel-opment of mega-landfills in Ohio, Pennsylvania, Michigan, Utah, and Virginia.

The process of choosing a community for waste export is by its very nature predatory. Crooks describes it as the search for "an internal Third World."[10] Long before local residents realize their area is under consid-eration, corporate planners establish a well-financed plan to push the project through the regulatory process. Locals count on provincial or state agencies to ensure that their best interests are protected as the process moves forward. They quickly learn otherwise. Communities aren't chosen because their land is ideal for a landfill, they are chosen because they aren't deemed to have the political or financial resources to fight back. As Heather Rogers puts it, they are targeted because they are considered "points of least resistance."[11]

During the 1980s various rural communities in Southern Ontario found themselves fighting pitched battles against the well-prepared Metro sales team. This is where Rhonda Hustler, who had come through a long waste battle in Warwick Township, entered the picture. She began to organize disparate rural resistance groups under an umbrella organization known as RAGE (Rural Action on Garbage and the Environment). Hustler played a significant role in helping unsuspecting communities realize the implications of getting caught up in the Metro Toronto process. In a letter to Englehart resident Kathy Martin, she warned of the danger of being reasonable—nice people end up with dumps:

> These consultants are all very nice and obliging, but they have been hired to make the process work in favour of Metro Toronto. In other words, they want us to co-operate and ultimately we give them our community for Metro garbage. Be careful of your comments . . . be very cautious and skeptical of everything they say.[12]

With the election of David Peterson's Liberal government in 1985, the rules for siting landfills in Ontario were modified. Toronto would be allowed to export garbage if it could find a "willing" host. On inspection, the Liberal government had changed the focus from finding a "suitable" site to a "willing" site. And once you were on the list of possible sites, good luck getting off. In 1989 the Liberal government overrode an environmental assessment decision that rejected a landfill site in Tiny Township near Midland. It was easier to keep Site 41 in play than to go back to the drawing board to find a more appropriate location. The community would fight the Site 41 landfill for the next twenty years. Such communities learned the hard way that inviting a waste proposal into the region was like inviting a vampire to cross the threshold. Once in, it seemed you could never get them to leave.

Gordon McGuinty desperately wanted to get on a list of acceptable sites. The provincial government announced a deadline of December 29, 1989, for submissions to be considered as a provincial landfill. Toronto was also looking to put together a short list for future alternatives to Keele Valley. McGuinty's problem was that he didn't have any money. His pitch to Adams Mine owner Dofasco (and partner Chevron) was simple—he asked for access to the Adams Mine with no money down. If Toronto didn't accept the bid, he would simply walk away. If McGuinty made it onto Toronto's short list, he would pay Dofasco/Chevron $1.2 million.[13] The mine owners had little to lose. And so on October 17, 1989, Chevron signed the deal with McGuinty in San Francisco.

He now needed a line of cash. There were four key partners—McGuinty, Lamarche, mining engineer Gilles Bernardin, and Sault Ste. Marie lawyer Gord Acton. They formed Notre Development Corporation and set out to find investors. They pitched the deal to northern investors like a classic penny stock mining deal: get in on the ground floor and, if the deal came through, everyone would be rolling in money.

And initially, the Adams Mine quickly moved up the ranks of credible options. Toronto short-listed a number of sites as a potential replacement for Keele Valley. Private developers in Lambton County were promoting some conventional small landfill options. Sites in Cayuga and Kent were also up for discussion. These locations were tempting, but none offered the massive expansion potential required by the city.

In the town of Orillia, a controversial incineration scheme was quickly going off the rails in the face of heavy local opposition. A second incineration option was being promoted in Kapuskasing, nearly 850 kilometres from Toronto. The sheer distance and the lack of an organized lobbying effort made it an unlikely choice. This left two sites—the Adams site and the Marmora Pit in Hastings Township—that were remarkably similar in nature.

The Marmora Pit was a six-hundred-foot quarry dug, like South Pit, into the surrounding groundwater table. As news of the Marmora plan spread, local opposition grew in leaps and bounds. At one meeting, over a thousand people came out to express their fears that using an abandoned mine would lead to serious groundwater contamination.

The Marmora option didn't last long. In a letter dated February 28, 1990, then minister of natural resources Lyn McLeod reassured local opponents that the water-filled mine was being defined as a "lake" and "to alter or destroy this habitat would require the authority of the federal minister of Fisheries and Oceans."[14]

In the letter, McLeod went on to raise concerns about the contamination of groundwater from the use of an open pit mine as a garbage dump. No similar letter was sent to residents in the north who were raising identical concerns about the Adams Mine. In fact, it would take fourteen more years and massive public opposition to force a subsequent Liberal administration to recognize that the water-filled Adams pits also meet the definition of a lake.

In 1989, news that Dofasco was shutting down its iron ore operations at Adams and Sherman Mine (near Temagami) sent shock waves through the region. Everyone knew that the shutdown of these mines spelled economic catastrophe for Timiskaming. Adams Mine was an economic linchpin for Kirkland Lake. Its sister operation, Sherman iron ore mine, anchored the economy of South Timiskaming. Together these mines supplied millions of tonnes of iron pellets to the steel mills of Hamilton, and provided a major freight contract for the struggling Ontario Northland Railway (ONR).

For the better part of a century the rich gold, iron, and silver mines of Timiskaming had made fortunes for faraway millionaires. The few remaining silver mines in Cobalt were shutting down. The area's once-mighty gold mines were limping along as diminished shadows of their former glory. And the forest industry had been hit by blockades and protests. Local people were worried. A region that had lived off the riches of the earth seemed to be facing a bleak future.

Little wonder that when Gordon McGuinty came knocking on the doors of the local town councils, he received a warm welcome. The Adams Mine wasn't in Kirkland Lake, it was eleven kilometres south in the Township of Boston. McGuinty, however, found his "willing hosts" in three regional town councils—Kirkland Lake, Larder Lake, and Englehart—that took it upon themselves to speak for the residents of Boston Township.

Long before any locals knew what was coming, McGuinty had lined up a strong base of political support. His strategy was to establish key "islands of truth"—claims that he would hold onto no matter what the opposition threw at him. The first island was to sell the project as a recycling centre, bringing badly needed jobs and new industry to the region. The second island was to tell people they didn't have to agree with the idea, they simply needed to support an environmental assessment on the project. As long as the public stayed focused on allowing an environmental assessment, the project could move ahead unhindered.

McGuinty advised local politicians to stick with this second island of truth as a way of avoiding political heat. "It was important to give the councils and the politicians the necessary buffer and the option to keep their distance from the project."[15] However, in pitching the Adams Mine project, McGuinty found that local politicians were just as willing as he was to step into the fray of promoting a mega-dump.

Putting People in a Box

Throughout the summer and fall of 1989, people in Kirkland Lake went about their business oblivious to the fact that, in North Bay, Notre

Development was preparing to lay siege to their town. Gordon McGuinty wasn't worried about the coming backlash. He knew it was inevitable. What Notre needed to do was to contain the local anger long enough to sign up Toronto as a partner. It was all about putting people in boxes. The first box was for the "antis." These were "unreasonable" people—those who could not be cajoled, intimidated, or fooled into supporting the project under any circumstances. This group would be defined at various points in the coming battle as "irresponsible" and "anti-job," or ridiculed as "eco-evangelists," "fanatics," and "terrorists."

The second box was for people who opposed the plan but who could be pressured into going along with the process. Locals were continually told that reasonable people should support an environmental assessment in order to be in a better position to decide whether or not to go ahead with the project. It wasn't mentioned that once the project was approved by an environmental assessment, the promoters wouldn't need to worry about local opinion any more. With an EA certificate in hand, the dump would be certain to move forward.

"Dissent and opposition are guaranteed," McGuinty wrote in his memoir. "The objective of managing the dissension is to contain it within a coalition of reasonable people . . . by creating a structure in which the totally unreasonable individuals (those who will never change, no matter what) are contained within the reasonable objections."[16]

To keep as many people as possible in this second box, Notre tried to define the language of the debate. Thus when they finally unveiled their plans to the public on November 29, 1989, a landfill wasn't even mentioned. Notre announced it was moving ahead with a very modest $70 million recycling facility at Adams Mine. Who could be opposed to recycling? It just so happened that this recycling operation included an onsite "solid waste facility."[17] Nobody in the know bothered to mention that this solid waste facility would dwarf any landfill ever built in Canada.

"The reality," McGuinty later wrote, "was that Toronto intended to develop all three pits [South, Central, and Peria] creating a total capacity of over 40 million tonnes . . . for a minimum of 30 years . . . up to 50 years."[18]

Recycling was never in the cards. There was no economic argument for shipping millions of tonnes of plastics and cardboard six hundred kilometres north to be separated and then returned to the city in other forms. As waste experts in Toronto knew full well, recycling is only economical when it happens at source. Nonetheless, locals were advised by town councillors and editorialists to keep focused on the recycling opportunities and to maintain an open mind when responding to this "forthright proposal."

"This is not to suggest the public should not question the new industry," opined a local editorial. "But the public must do so in a reasonable fashion . . . not jumping to conclusions or reacting in a negative way based solely on vague preconceptions."[19]

Thus, it was okay to ask questions. What wasn't okay was to say anything that could damage a potential "gold mine" in its early stages. Residents were warned not to refer to "Toronto garbage" because, as one town councillor stated, it "gives people the wrong idea."[20] Instead, the preferred term was "refuse disposal."

The region was facing a very precarious future and there was enormous pressure on concerned residents not to be seen damaging a potential future industry. Kirkland Lake mayor Joe Mavrinac warned residents that if there was "negative reactionary [behaviour] . . . the potential for a billion dollar industry could slip through our fingers."[21]

With the plan unveiled, McGuinty moved quickly to throw potential opponents off their game. He set up meetings with any group or person that might come out against him. Seventeen-year-old Megan Leslie was shocked when the president of Notre Development asked to meet with her high school environmental group. He even donated to her fundraising effort to pay for a development trip overseas.

"He was lobbying us and we were teenagers," recalls Leslie, who is now environment critic for the federal New Democratic Party. "I can't believe how effective he was in making us feel that we should be more reasonable and careful when talking about the issue."

Like him or hate him, people had to admit that Gordon McGuinty had moxy. He took his sales pitch to all comers. At an early public meeting with Laurentian University geology professor David Pearson, he boasted that the pit exceeded provincial environmental guidelines by "five to ten times." He had no studies to back up this claim. He also assured residents (many of whom had relatives working at the mine) that the pit walls were "impermeable."

Pearson politely disagreed. "The walls look thoroughly shattered, and not impermeable to me," he stated.[22]

But McGuinty had his line and he hammered it home again and again. He later wrote: "During a meeting it is important to manage the dynamics of the audience . . . a good strategy is to let people talk themselves out. . . . Never leave the speaker's platform. . . . no matter how hostile the meeting . . . make a point of staying until the protesters have walked out."[23]

McGuinty showed up at any meeting, whether it was organized by the pro or con side. He would come with his sidekick Elizabeth Fournier, who rarely spoke at meetings. Nevertheless, she seemed to me as solid as a gun moll made up like Tammy Faye Bakker. Neither McGuinty nor Fournier blinked. If people ranted about garbage, McGuinty spoke about the merits of recycling.

At an early public forum, resident Chris Beeson challenged McGuinty's recycling sales pitch: "It sounds like a mega-dump to me."

McGuinty's response was categorical. "We're not interested in accepting anybody's waste without a recycling plant."[24]

As Notre had anticipated, a group of local professionals stepped forward to oppose the project. They called themselves the Responsible Environmental and Economic Prosperity Association (REEPA). The founders of the group had been careful to select key respected leaders in the community as spokespeople. McGuinty publicly welcomed this fledgling group and reassured them that they had a "tremendous role" to play in the process. But the welcome mat didn't stay out for long. Before REEPA was even out of the gate, the pro-dump forces quickly moved onto the offensive.

REEPA spokesperson John Epps came under withering public attack. The pro-dump reeve of Larder Lake, David Oehring, accused Epps of being "insulting and irresponsible." McGuinty said Epps was trying to "confuse" local residents. Pro-dump councillors openly questioned Epps's motives. Clearly thrown off by this display of venom, Dr. Epps wrote a long letter to the local paper reminding local residents that he was a "responsible" member of the community. He listed his public service as a doctor, Boy Scout leader, church elder, and even as a "volunteer physician" on the annual Santa Claus Express train for children.[25]

REEPA member William Durocher was attacked publicly for asking the Kirkland Lake Council to withhold support for the project until after the results of an environmental assessment. McGuinty accused Dr. Durocher of waging a campaign of "misinformation."

"You're writing those letters to confuse the population, to put pressure on this council and that isn't fair," McGuinty suggested. Durocher was then lectured on his obligation to speak from a basis of "responsibility."[26]

Kirkland Lake councillor Sue Gamble also came under fire when she joined REEPA. She was attacked at council meetings and in the press for "stalling for time" and being "hypocritical," or "massaging" her ego in public by raising questions about the process. Gamble, a tough Kirkland Laker who worked in mining exploration, gave back as good as she got. "The issue," she wrote in a letter to the paper, "is not to massage my ego, the issue is 25 million tonnes of Toronto garbage."[27]

Gamble accused council of abandoning its obligation to protect the public interest. "Unfortunately normal citizens have to band together to fill a void left by elected officials in providing opposition," she said.

The public attacks on REEPA gave other small-town professionals pause for thought as to whether they should get caught up in the fight.

REEPA goes to Metro Council. 1993 protest in Toronto with REEPA members (left to right) Martha McSherry, Lynne Epps, John Epps, Edna Davis. PHOTO: courtesy of Martha McSherry

Perhaps it was better to keep their heads low. For those who had taken a stand, energy that should have been spent pointing out serious flaws in the dump proposal was spent responding to accusations about their motives. Yet from the beginning, REEPA members like Martha McSherry and Edna Davis were tenacious in keeping the issue focused on the facts and the obvious problems of using the Adams Mine as a dump.

One of the first groups McGuinty asked to meet with was VOME (Victims of Mining Environment)—a group of mining widows who fought for compensation for victims of silicosis. VOME had recently been in the press because of their public opposition to importing radioactive waste to the north.

In the run-up to the meeting with Notre, the members of VOME found themselves fending off attacks from local councillors who accused them of being "anti-job." VOME resident Joan Hodgins was thrown on the defensive. "Our Town council has said that since we're against radioactive waste we're against jobs. We're not against jobs." To show she wasn't "unreasonable," Hodgins tried to extend the olive branch: "If this [the Adams Mine project] is environmentally safe and good clean industry, that's something we're going to have to consider."[28]

Local media were quick to announce that VOME was giving thumbs up to the project. McGuinty told the press he was pleasantly surprised by their "open mind," especially since he had been warned that they were "placard carrying" protesters.

Hodgins wasn't mollified for long, and like many others, moved from the reasonable to the unreasonable camp fairly quickly. At a subsequent public meeting, she would attack McGuinty's plan publicly: "Southern Ontario has raped the north for years. They have taken our gold, timber and children. Now they want to repay us with garbage."[29]

Strong words, but ones that McGuinty could easily shrug off. By the time the women of VOME began to speak out, the Adams Mine project was already established on Toronto's short list of ten possible sites because the cooperation of Kirkland Lake, Larder Lake, and Englehart town councils gave it "willing host" status.

The First Skirmish

Snowflakes were falling as the miners stepped out from the main office building of Sherman iron ore mine. In a grim procession, as a piper played "Amazing Grace," they marched in their workboots and hard hats to a hill overlooking the main pit. Mine manager Syd Bartlett stepped forward and said a few words.

"It's been a good run," he said, simply. "You've been a good gang, but now it's over."

And with that, a miner played the last post and the Canadian flag was lowered from the mast for the last time. Sherman and Adams mines closed on March 31, 1990.[30]

As the last post was sounding over a now dead iron mine, a group of northerners were in Toronto firing the first shot of the Adams Mine war. When Metro chair Alan Tonks stepped out of the elevator at City Hall for another day of work, he was met by a group of protesters presenting him with a symbolic bag of garbage. "We're drawing the line in the sand," Elk Lake resident Terry Graves told Tonks. "We're saying the north is not open for southern garbage."

Fran Patterson, who had driven down from the rural Kenabeek region in central Timiskaming, thrust a five-thousand-name petition at Tonks. "We will not be known as the garbage capital of Ontario," she declared.

Tonks was caught off guard. Not only had these protesters jumped him at work, but they had ensured that provincial media were there to witness the confrontation. They may have been from the northern back-woods, but they weren't political bumpkins.

Graves and Patterson were members of the Temiskaming Environ-mental Action Committee (TEAC), the organized face of McGuinty's "unreasonable" people. TEAC drew its membership from the region's small but innovative countercultural community. Some members, like Joe Muething and Kathy Martin, had come to the area from the United States to escape the Vietnam War. Others, like Fran and Dave Patterson and Ambrose Raftis, came north as youthful hippie adventurers.

TEAC had been active in the region since 1979, and members had cut their teeth on numerous environmental fights. They had fought Agent Orange–type herbicides in cutovers and organized against nuclear waste being sited in Elk Lake. Many had been active in the recent logging blockades against the threatened white pine forests in Temagami. They weren't neophytes to activism. They understood that getting bogged down in a promoter-driven process was a ticket to failure—hence their determination to move the battle to the decision-makers at Toronto City Hall and the provincial legislature at Queen's Park. There they found many willing allies.

Among the progressive councillors at Toronto City Hall, the notion of hauling garbage six hundred kilometres to dump in an environmentally questionable site served as a wake-up call. As long as the city could look to the northern hinterlands for disposal, local politicians would not get serious about investing in recycling and waste diversion initiatives. TEAC quickly made alliances with members of Toronto Council including Jack Layton.

At the provincial level, the fight to "protect the north" was taken up by the opposition New Democrats. The symbolism of turning the north into Toronto's garbage dump touched a very deep and emotional chord. The north was the land of the Group of Seven. Dumping waste there was a damning symbol of the failure of urban society to deal with its growing appetite for consumption.

In the north, the idea of filling the Adams Mine with garbage had equally symbolic resonance. Northerners have traditionally felt they are little more than a resource colony of a disinterested urban south. The Adams Mine project appeared at a time when the north was losing political and economic ground. In local coffee shops, the plan stirred long-held feelings of resentment and alienation. People remembered how Kirkland Lake's gold mines had helped keep Ontario afloat during the Depression. Now most of the big mines were shutting down, and it seemed that hardrock mining in the north was a sunset industry. The sense of abandonment was profound: *We've given our raw materials—lumber, gold, copper, and hydro—to the south, and they want to ship us their garbage in return.*

The big question was how this sense of regional resentment would play in the coming fight over the Adams Mine. The Temagami logging blockade had generated deep-seated resentment among many locals who felt that "outsiders" (including TEAC) were undermining their way of life.

The promoters of the project had banked on the insecurity of this eroding blue-collar base to drive a wedge between laid-off miners and the "hippie" environmentalists of TEAC. But waste wars are not like other environmental fights, because they are fundamentally rooted in class. People in the north instinctively knew that they were being targeted because they were considered political have-nots. The sense of having been exploited for the benefit of distant millionaires ran very deep in the psyche of the region. And so it is not surprising that many blue-collar folk were more than willing to side with TEAC's confrontational approach to the dump scheme.

Norm MacDonald was typical of this early crossover. As a hardrock miner, MacDonald was well versed in the issues of groundwater flowing through fractured rock. He saw the plan as a reckless scheme and began going door to door gathering signatures to stop the dump. Over the next fifteen years, Norm and his wife, Brenda, never wavered in their determination. They were among the first of many working-class people who felt at home with the more militant environmentalist tactics of TEAC.

Queen's Park Steps In

On September 6, 1990, Bob Rae's New Democratic Party swept into power with a majority government. Newly installed environment minister Ruth Grier made no secret of her distaste for the plan to ship urban waste to the Canadian Shield. Local dump opponents from REEPA and TEAC headed to Toronto to press the newly elected provincial government to stop the Adams Mine. They had in their hands local surveys and petitions that showed "overwhelming opposition" to the Notre plan.

The Notre supporters were in trouble. Unless they could quickly show grassroots support, they feared the plan would be deep-sixed.

Blue-collar and rural residents in Timiskaming became radicalized early on in the process.

A local editorial pleaded for a "yes petition." "There are petitions circulating opposing the Adams Mine proposal. Why are there no petitions in favour?"[31]

Notre's response was to help create a citizens' group that could promote the project as a nominally independent grassroots organization—an established waste industry tactic that, now referred to as astroturfing, has recently been picked up by the oil industry. The organization was hatched at a private dinner put together by Notre Development. The guest speaker for the event was an amiable fellow, George Duncan, who ran the local assay laboratory.

"What are we, nuts? We're saying 'no' to the best thing that could happen to Kirkland Lake," Dr. Duncan told fellow dump supporters and investors. In speaking to the press, he admitted he had a vested interest, through his work with the assay lab, in ensuring the success of the landfill.[32] Nonetheless, he became the public face of FACTS (Fair and Corroborated True Study)—a group that would provide the "grassroots" support to challenge the provincial government's opposition to Notre's plan.

But the FACTS committee didn't fool anyone at Queen's Park. The fledgling opposition in Timiskaming had out-organized Notre, and they had the ear of the new government. Soon after coming to power, the New Democrats overruled the Toronto selection process by establishing a provincial body to decide appropriate sites for the waste of the city and the surrounding Greater Toronto Area. The Interim Waste Authority (IWA) took its task seriously. Minister Grier also established the Waste Reduction Office (WRO) to move the province forward on garbage reduction and recycling strategies.

The media and opposition politicians ridiculed such ideas as a costly "boondoggle." David Lewis Stein of *The Toronto Star* compared these efforts at waste diversion to the Spanish Inquisition: "I fear the NDP is now listening to people who want to save the planet with the same punishing fervour that an earlier generation of zealots showed when they saved immortal souls by burning heretics at the stake."[33] *Star* writer Royson

James said Grier's opponents believed she was creating a "garbage apocalypse."[34]

At Metro Council, there was little desire to work with the NDP on
finding credible waste alternatives. Early on, the key players at City Hall
decided to bide their time, believing that they were facing a single-term
provincial government. And thus, while local opponents of the Adams
Mine went back to their day-to-day lives, Notre got down to work to
put a much more comprehensive plan in place. They signed on waste
giant BFI as a key partner. The Ontario Northland Railway joined as well.
Metro Toronto kicked in $4 million to fund the studies needed to move
the project forward. Gordon McGuinty may have lost round one, but he
was determined to be ready when the bell sounded for round two.

The biggest ace in McGuinty's hand was the fact that his friend Mike
Harris had been voted leader of the provincial Progressive Conservative party. McGuinty was an old skiing and golf buddy of Harris. He had
worked on Harris's first election campaign and was present at North Bay's
Davedi Club the night that Harris was chosen as leader of the Progressive
Conservatives. Harris's campaign manager, Barb Minogue, was an investor in the Adams Mine.

In 1991, Harris and McGuinty met with the key players of the Adams
Mine at Bigliardi's steakhouse in Toronto. Joining them at this meeting
was Kirkland Lake mayor Joe Mavrinac, Toronto Works commissioner
Bob Ferguson, Toronto councillor Joan King, and investor/friend Peter
Minogue (husband of Barb Minogue).[35] The meeting over steak and
wine laid out the plans for moving quickly to bring the Adams Mine to
fruition once the Rae government was defeated. None of the main players at the dinner noticed that the man sitting at the table beside them was
TEAC activist Terry Graves. As Graves listened in to the strategy, he realized how key the role of Mike Harris was to the whole endeavour. If the
Progressive Conservatives won the next election, Adams Mine was going
to be on the top of their agenda.

2

Invasion of the
Process Snatchers
1995

The Tories won every seat in the band of 17 affluent, antiseptic ridings which separate Toronto from the great unwashed. They won precisely zero seats north of Highway 17.

During the election Harris promised that there would be no mega-dumps in barbeque country. And he knows Toronto won't suck its own incineration smoke. He also knows about three million voters in the Greater Toronto Area would nominate him for sainthood if he could make 40 million tonnes of garbage disappear in, say, an abandoned mine near Kirkland Lake.

— "Split Level Victory," *HighGrader Magazine*, July 1995

Do you know how you lead a bull to the slaughterhouse? You limit its options. You move it from the field, into the pen and then onto the back of the truck by making it follow a path where it has no other choice but to take the next step. And the last decision it makes is onto the back of the truck. Wake up people—this is exactly what Metro Toronto is doing to us.

— Farmer at a public meeting in Earlton, 1995

Round Two

F OUR YEARS after the steak dinner at Bigliardi's, Mike Harris turned the political landscape of Ontario upside down. The Common Sense Revolution gave moderate Ontario a crash course in the roughshod, hot-button politics common to the Republican states south of the border. No one saw it coming. But in the months leading up to the historic 1995 election, the people of Timiskaming had an advanced peek at the upheaval about to be unleashed by Mike Harris. Take, for example, the two hundred people gathered in the Legion Hall in the relatively conservative town of Englehart, Ontario, on a warm night in May. As nervous Ontario Provincial Police officers looked on, the locals moved to the verge of open confrontation.

It was in the dying days of the Bob Rae government, and Metro Works officials had showed up in Timiskaming anticipating big, big changes on the provincial scene. Toronto Council was thumbing its nose at the Interim Waste Authority, which forbade them from shipping garbage north. Rather than wait for the upcoming election to open up their options, they decided to jump-start the process of siting the Adams Mine. Englehart, a railway town in the heart of Timiskaming's small Bible belt, was one of the three "willing host" communities that supported the project. The Adams Mine promoters were promising garbage as a lifeline for the struggling Ontario Northland rail line. But if Metro Toronto expected a warm welcome from the people of Englehart, it was seriously mistaken.

Metro officials had set up the meeting to select representatives for the regional Public Liaison Committee (PLC) being established in preparation for an environmental assessment on the Adams Mine. Metro Works proposed establishing a fifteen-person team to participate in the public review committee. Many of the seats had already been guaranteed to the three local councils and to economic development interests that favoured the mine. The remaining seats were to be elected positions chosen at public forums in Englehart, Round Lake, Larder Lake, and Kirkland Lake.

The problem with the plan was that a large section of Timiskaming's twenty-six townships were excluded from the process.

The people in the Englehart Legion felt as if they had been taken hostage in their own town. Who the hell was Metro Toronto to dictate the rules of engagement to them? Why was Toronto deciding who was allowed at the table and who wasn't? It reeked of a fixed process. As Metro Works representative Lawson Oates patiently explained the ground rules, the audience became increasingly restive. At one point, Patricia Hewitt stood up to confront Oates. "This isn't a fair process and we are going to stop it."

Hewitt came from the picturesque farming community of Thornloe, one of the municipalities that had been excluded from the PLC. If Toronto didn't want Thornloe's participation, too damned bad. Hewitt, a striking young woman with a firecracker personality, turned to the crowd and asked if they would nominate her to sit at the table. The crowd cheered wildly. Oates told her to sit down or the police would forcibly remove her.

It wasn't the first time Metro officials had used the threat of police at local meetings, but Hewitt wasn't intimidated. "You might ask me to leave, Mr. Oates, but that doesn't mean I'll comply."

As Oates motioned to two OPP officers to remove Hewitt, other farm women stood up and challenged the police to try and drag them out as well. For a moment it appeared as if Metro's carefully controlled meeting was going to deteriorate into an old-fashioned donnybrook. But the police, deciding that discretion was the better part of valour, stepped back, leaving Oates to carry on as best he could.[1]

Englehart was not the kind of town where people challenged the local police to a showdown. But the anger that spilled over in the Legion Hall was an indication that something seismic was happening in rural Timiskaming.

From the earliest days of the process, the fight centred on the water. South Pit sat three hundred feet in the water table.[2] The promoters promised that as long as water flowed into the pit, a massive pumping system could prevent leachate from flowing out. The farmers and miners in Englehart knew all about water flows and the reliability of pumps. Their livelihood depended on such practical knowledge. Many in the hall had worked in the pits, and they knew the condition of the pit walls. They looked incredulously at the slick consultants hired by Notre Development who blandly assured them that the site was ideal. Not to worry, Notre told locals, they would pump and monitor the pits for a thousand years after the dump had closed.[3]

Sure. Anyone in the region could point to a hundred plus abandoned mine properties dotting the hills from Cobalt to Kirkland Lake that were left to ooze arsenic and other contaminants the minute the local mining company stopped making money. And yet Metro Toronto was here telling them to disregard everything they knew about rock, groundwater, and pumping. Many in the hall wanted nothing to do with the process. They wanted Metro to get the hell out of town.

A public planning process is a carefully scripted event that limits the options of reluctant locals. But by setting up a process that straddled a provincial election, Metro officials made a number of tactical errors. For one, they misjudged the speed of the backlash. Thus, by the time the election was called in May 1995, Adams Mine had been pushed to the forefront of attention in the region.

If the promoter tries to narrow the options through the public consultation period, the opposition aims to make the promoter respond to a citizen-driven initiative. The election provided the perfect opportunity. Given that Ontario Conservative leader Mike Harris was a bullish promoter of the Adams Mine, the election became an alternative venue for a debate on the issues that Metro Toronto had been hoping to contain.

Ambrose Raftis, a local environmentalist, presented himself as a candidate for the NDP and quickly turned the election in Timiskaming–Cochrane into a referendum on the Adams Mine. With his wire-rimmed glasses and mad-scientist hair, Raftis became a lightning rod for both proponents and opponents of the project.

Raftis used the campaign as a pulpit to publicly trash what he called a "massive experiment" with the groundwater of Timiskaming. In the middle of the election, he released his own "Raftis Report" that presented in vivid simplicity how easily leachate could escape through the fractured pit walls into the surrounding farm belt.

Raftis drove his opponents crazy. He derailed the carefully scripted messaging from Metro Toronto. He also forced his political opponents to take a stand. Liberal MPP David Ramsay, who had entered the election as a supporter of the Adams Mine project, sensed the change in the political winds and came out very strongly mid-election against the dump.

On June 7, 1995, with the election all but in the bag, premier-elect Harris finally landed in Timiskaming. He was on a last-minute barnstorming tour through the north, intended to provide provincial media with a friendly photo op of Northern Ontario's most successful politician returning to his roots. But Harris, the man who promised to make the Adams Mine a reality, flew straight into confrontation. As his plane landed at Earlton airport, the tarmac was surrounded by angry locals with farm machinery and manure spreaders. They blocked the tarmac and jostled angrily with local Conservative volunteers. Jim Crorkin, an expat American carpenter, stood alongside Earlton farmer Mary Loranger. She was backed by a cross-section of the tightly knit francophone farming clans—the Ethiers, Gauthiers, and Rivards. "We're farmers not garbage pickers," she shouted out defiantly to the incoming premier.[4]

One of their signs read "No Toronto Garbage or There Will Be a Revolution." This crowd hadn't come to plead with Harris. They were sending a message: they would fight like hell to stop him.

Mike Harris running the gauntlet through a crowd of angry protesters could have provided the provincial media with the perfect image to define what was about to become the most divisive government in Ontario history. But the journalists on board the campaign plane took a pass on covering this first skirmish of the Common Sense Revolution. The garbage battle of Timiskaming wasn't part of their storyline.

On the eve of the Common Sense Revolution, Mike Harris is confronted by Timiskaming resident Jim Crorkin. Earlton airport, June 7, 1995.

HighGrader Magazine, a publication Brit Griffin and I had started earlier that year to look at resource and culture issues from a northern perspective, was more than willing to fill the gap. The Adams Mine garbage fight seemed tailor-made for our publication. We knew that the Harris years were going to be controversial. Our magazine was born in exciting times. But, as I was soon to learn, no one sits on the sidelines in a waste war. The Adams Mine fight quickly absorbed our focus and energy. In no time at all, I was drawn across the divide from journalist to activist.

Despite the showdown at Earlton airport, Harris took the Ontario election by a landslide. Ramsay's decision to come out strongly against the Adams Mine helped him secure the riding of Timiskaming–Cochrane for the Liberals. Raftis received only 16 per cent of the vote, but in its year-end round up of news, *The Temiskaming Speaker* identified him as a "perfect example of losing the election but winning the campaign."

Harris didn't sweat the fact that he had been shut out of Northern Ontario. The Common Sense Revolution had been focused on winning the suburban "905" belt surrounding Toronto (a region popularly referred to by its area code, in contrast to Toronto's "416"). In a strategy that would later be imitated at the national level by Stephen Harper and municipally by Toronto's Rob Ford, Harris played on the politics of suburban backlash. Unlike the centrist Progressive Conservative governments of the past, Harris stoked suburban anger by promising action like abandoning photo radar, promoting tax cuts, and shutting down proposed landfill developments in suburbia. The suburbs heard the message loud and clear, and gave him the largest majority in postwar Ontario history.

Little wonder that his very first act as premier was to kill the Interim Waste Authority and the Waste Reduction Office, effectively giving the green light to the Adams Mine.[5] In the process, Harris eliminated the three environmentally sound sites that had been identified for handling waste in Vaughan, Peel, and Durham regions. Media noted that the move was the ultimate victory of NIMBYism in "Tory strongholds." Suburban 905 now had a "veto" over any future landfills.[6] "The community will be dancing in the streets. We are excited as hell," said Mario Ferri, president of a local Vaughan group opposed to the proposed Toronto site.[7]

The obvious question was, where would the garbage go? John Aker, chair of the Durham Region Works Committee, didn't care. "Ship it north or ship it south," he said bluntly.[8] The days when Oshawa would look after its own garbage were over.

Forgotten in the suburban giddiness about sinking the IWA and the WRO was the fact that four years of work and $80 million in technical work to identify regional solutions were being flushed down the toilet. Nobody seemed interested in the red flags that had been raised about the Adams Mine. In particular, a study by the Ontario Treasury Ministry warned that, even in the best-case scenario, the Adams Mine was going to cost the city of Toronto $650 million more than any local or regional option.

In the north, no one was surprised by the speed at which Harris moved. "Everyone recognizes that Mike Harris and Gordon McGuinty are close personal friends," stated TEAC leader Terry Graves. "We've been expecting this announcement."9

McGuinty dismissed comments about his friendship with the premier as an "insult" to the integrity of both men. McGuinty was always adamant that their friendship involved nothing more than the occasional game of golf. But Harris would be as good as his election promise—he was determined to make the Adams Mine dump a reality.

Hot Night at the Bon Air

During the election, Ambrose Raftis had caused the Adams Mine promoters a great deal of havoc. But the havoc wasn't over, and neither was the payback. Four days after the election of Harris, Metro Works held the first formal meeting of the Public Liaison Committee at the Bon Air inn in Kirkland Lake. A large crowd gathered to get their first view of the fifteen elected and appointed representatives entrusted with the job of reviewing the merits and demerits of the project. The crowd was overwhelmingly made up of anti-dump activists.

Before the meeting got under way, police moved in and removed Dr. Kelly Kramp and Don Wright, who had been "elected" by residents in townships that had been excluded from the process. As he was being led away by the police, Wright called out to the crowd, "My people are not being represented. The only people represented here are people for Metro Toronto."

The crowd heckled the police as well as interim chair Andy Pollock of Metro Works. A police officer stepped into the crowd to tell two women, Eva Graves and Brennain Lloyd, to be quiet or they would be removed.

Ambrose Raftis was sitting beside them. He asked the officer if freedom of speech was still allowed in this country. The officer put his hand on Raftis's shoulder, and as soon as the officer touched him, Raftis flew off his chair and landed on the ground. (Eyewitness accounts vary as to whether Raftis fell or was self-propelled when the police touched him.) People started shouting at the police. The embarrassed officer didn't react very well. He grabbed Raftis and dragged him out of the meeting in a chokehold.

Local news reporter Walter Franczyk captured the image of the police choking Raftis and the photograph went on to win a National Press Award.[10] The Raftis photo played to the sense of a region being forced into a process against its will. For Metro, the night went downhill from there.

A local health care official, PLC member Elizabeth Denton, challenged the police. "Why was he fingered. It looked like a set up. The force the police used on Mr. Raftis was disgusting. Mr. McGuinty was louder [during the meeting] than Mr. Raftis. I was louder than Mr. Raftis. When people go to meetings should we be expected to be arrested and thrown in jail?"[11]

The chokehold seemed to symbolize the skewed process that had led to the fifteen people around the table being chosen. A number of the seats had been reserved for municipal councils and economic development organizations that supported the project. The opposition members came from people elected in local community town halls undertaken by Metro Works. Also sitting at the table was Toronto lawyer Rob Power, who had been hired to represent the interests of the three "host" communities. As the meeting got under way, Powers and the dump opponents on the PLC began to scuffle over the ground rules.

A Kirkland Lake prospector, PLC member George Mangotich, wanted to know why the environmental group TEAC wasn't allowed to sit at the table, when the Notre-associated FACTS group had representation. "Why should Metro make all the rules? This is Northern Ontario and we should make our own rules."

Mangotich wouldn't drop the issue and Power, showing his frustration, challenged him. "From what I'm hearing, you are saying 'thank you

Metro for coming here, but we would really like to move on with our own committee process.'"[12]

Mangotich didn't hesitate. "You are making all the rules. I don't want these rules."

Power had become a familiar face at local town halls. At his first public meeting, the Toronto lawyer presented himself as on the side of the people of Timiskaming. "We want our friends from Metro to understand how important it is do the job right," he reassured locals.[13] But the PLC members hadn't been told that Power was intimately involved with the Conservative power structure as well as with Notre Development. He had been an adviser to Harris on changing the Environmental Assessment Act, and had worked with McGuinty on setting up the deal with BFI.

Joe Muething, who was elected to the PLC to represent the rural region of Charlton-Dack, wasn't reassured by Power's positive message. "The first time I saw him I thought he looked like a young Richard Nixon," Muething recalls.

The meeting at the Bon Air dragged on under the suspicious eyes of a loud and hostile anti-dump crowd. Metro Works representatives were clearly rattled by both the crowd and the tenacity of the anti-dump members who formed a block around Muething, Mangotich, Denton, and John Nychuk. Two hours into the meeting, interim chair Andy Pollock attempted to introduce John Finn of Englehart, who had been chosen by Metro as the "independent" chair for the process. As Finn was to step forward to accept his post, John Vanthof, a last-minute addition to the PLC, spoke up.

The Temiskaming Federation of Agriculture (TFA), which Vanthof represented, had originally been excluded from the process. But responding to widespread pressure, McGuinty and Power had invited Vanthof to a screening interview the night before. The polite young farmer stated that his only interest was whether the dump would affect farmers' water supply, and McGuinty declared him a "reasonable" candidate for inclusion on the PLC.

"Mr. Pollock," said Vanthof, "I don't know how you do things in Toronto but up here we tend to pick our chairs democratically."

The pro-dump forces scrambled for a response. Up until that moment Vanthof had been an unknown quality to both the pro and the anti forces gathered at the table. "Can we at least hear from Mr. Finn?" pleaded Pollock. "Well that wouldn't be fair to the rest of the candidates that we might put forward," Vanthof replied.

Realizing he didn't have the numbers to force Mr. Finn's appointment, Pollock had to concede that the choice of a chair would be dealt with at the next meeting. The Metro team then moved to introduce the consultant team, Gartner Lee, who would provide peer review support for the committee.

"This landfill is a unique project," explained Power. "It requires a wide range of special skills. In the Province of Ontario, there is not a lot of consulting engineering firms that have the expertise in the wide range of issues you have raised at your public meeting. Gartner Lee will give you some sense in understanding the issues."[14]

This was all fine, Vanthof replied, but shouldn't the PLC pick its own consultant? Larder Lake representative David Oehring blew up at Vanthof. "First you insulted the man put up to be chair and now you're insulting a highly respected hydrology firm."

Vanthof, keeping up the friendly, folksy manner replied, "I'm not trying to insult anybody but I have to go back to a meeting of 300 farmers and they will ask how did you select the independent consultant? Am I to say, Robert Power recommended it, no other names were given and we took his word for it?"

Once again, the Metro plan had been shut down.

This initial meeting lasted nearly five and a half hours. As Ambrose Raftis cooled his heals at the Kirkland Lake jail, Rob Power and the Metro team realized that a potentially more serious adversary had arisen in the form of farm leader John Vanthof. He may have lacked the professional credentials of Notre's high-priced consultants, but he was well educated in the facts of business life. In high school, he had been considered an ideal candidate for university, but he quit school to help his father run the family farm. When his father was killed in a tractor accident, Vanthof took full control of the dairy operation. He was good at business and quickly emerged as an eloquent spokesperson for his fellow farmers.

Vanthof had gone to the initial meeting ready to work with the process, but he soon realized that Metro had just one goal—getting the project approved regardless of its shortcomings. Now the MPP for Timiskaming–Cochrane, Vanthof says the first PLC meeting was a political eye opener for him. "I thought initially that maybe these guys do know what they're talking about. Maybe they do have a plan. But when I saw the procedural games they were playing, I thought, what is going on here? I knew we were being bullshitted, and that's the way they continued throughout the entire process. They fed us bullshit every step of the way."

As the PLC process dragged on into the summer, Vanthof became increasingly outspoken in his concerns. The farmers wanted assurances that leachate would not escape through the badly fractured pit walls and contaminate the underground aquifers that fed their farms. But no efforts had been made to map or track whether the water flowing in South Pit was part of a larger regional aquifer. It was all conjecture.

Vanthof believes the engineers and hydrogeologists simply hadn't done their homework. "At any given meeting, there were old mining guys at the back of the room who would ask clear, detailed questions about water flow and rock fractures, and the consultants didn't have an answer for them. If they couldn't answer what was actually happening now in terms of ground flow, how were they in any position to predict what was going to happen hundreds of years from now?"

Timiskaming resident John Goodwin, for example, came to numerous PLC meetings to ask why the iron content in his well had skyrocketed once the pumps at South Pit had been turned off.[15] If the Adams Mine was not connected to surrounding aquifers, why did the wells in the region south of the mine have such dramatic changes in water quality once the mine pumps stopped running? Goodwin wasn't the only resident unsatisfied by the bland assurances coming from the consultants.

"Groundwater doesn't respect ignorance and neither do the people of Timiskaming," said Vanthof at a meeting with Notre's consultants in Earlton. "The answers from the consultants haven't gotten better, just longer."

As trust deteriorated, the Temiskaming Federation of Agriculture announced they were going to take a leadership role in opposing the project. Rob Power denounced the move as a "slap in the face" and vowed that the farmers' continued presence on the PLC would be "thoroughly investigated."

. "It's like we opened the door to our house and they walked away with our economic opportunity. Who are they to come to the northern part of the district and take away our economic opportunity?"[16] He then fired off a twelve-point letter of accusation against farm leaders Gary Struthers and John Vanthof. The letter accused the TFA of "organizing through closed door meetings, a group of individuals to oppose the EA process."[17]

If the letter was supposed to intimidate the farmers, it had the opposite effect. In a reply sent the same day, Struthers blew Power off:

> While I don't feel compelled to explain my thought processes to you . . . being asked to accept only the risks associated with this proposal (placing in jeopardy a $30 million a year industry) while the municipalities you represent receive the benefits ($1 million a year), seems like a logical reason to oppose the project. . . . You should understand that I generally don't take well to threats and intimidation.[18]

A Region at War

The PLC process was supposed to reassure the people of Timiskaming that all due diligence was being done regarding the Adams Mine proposal. But those who watched the proceedings were beginning to believe that the outcome was already determined. The representatives from Metro weren't dishonest, they were simply following the standard battle plan of any so-called public consultation process. Whether you are dealing with a dump, an oil and gas project, or major municipal rezoning, public participation is just one more box that must be ticked off as the process rolls along.

The process isn't there to take direction from the public and is often not set up to respond to the legitimate problems that are brought forward. All too often, public consultation is there to legitimize the final outcome. If the public doesn't participate, then the proponents can claim there was little opposition. Those that do participate are expected to invest a great deal of their time, their emotions, and their hopes in an exercise that is often little more than a "heads I win, tails you lose" game.

The PLC members took their work seriously and dutifully attempted to work through the numerous questions surrounding the project. However, as the process wore on, many in the public began to believe that the Metro planners and the hired consultants were not interested in addressing the numerous problems being raised.

Stan Gorzalczynski, a local technologist who attended all the meetings, wrote about his frustration in a letter to the local media:

> It has become apparent that Metro Works is not spending three million dollars to evaluate the pit but is instead spending this money to blur the facts already known. I find that each public meeting is producing a considerable number of extreme opponents to this proposal, regardless of what community it is held in.[19]

Locals began to feel that the fix was already in. This is what led to the radicalization of a very moderate rural population. People faced a stark choice: either you were willing to go along with the gamble or you were going to fight to stop it. There was no middle ground, no compromise.

By late summer 1995, the either-or division cut right through the region. Within Kirkland Lake Town Council, the fault lines were drawn between two councillors—Richard Denton and Bill Enouy. Dr. Denton was a family practitioner who, with his stylish fedora, ascot, and Quaker beard, seemed as if he has stepped out of another time. He had been one of the first members of the local environmental group REEPA.

Facing off against him was teacher and hockey coach Bill Enouy. Enouy played politics like he played Kirkland Lake–style hockey—when the team is under fire you drop the gloves. Kirkland Lake had been under fire for years with job losses and the steady bleed-off of families. The town had been built around the famed Mile of Gold, with seven operating mines that had attracted labouring families from across Canada and Europe. That was a long time ago. If waste was the only new industry on the horizon, Enouy was willing to fight for the option.

Denton and Enouy were both passionate boosters of their town, but the Adams Mine proposal made any kind of shared vision impossible. Across the region, long-standing social norms were fraying badly. Nowhere was the fight nastier than in the conflict between MPP David Ramsay and Kirkland Lake mayor Joe Mavrinac.

Mavrinac was a tough, old, ward-boss-style politician. Since 1990, he had been pushing back against locals who demanded a referendum on the project. Ramsay had championed the right of locals to have a say. He used his MPP's budget to promote local surveys that showed huge opposition to the project. Ramsay's support of the referendum became a source of growing friction with Mavrinac's council.

On August 10, 1995, Ramsay held a press conference in Kirkland Lake and accused Mayor Mavrinac of committing "fraud" by lying to local people. At issue was a promise made during the 1991 municipal election to hold a referendum on the controversial project. Ramsay called out Mavrinac for failing to keep this promise. Ramsay's language was confrontational. "I don't like it when a politician lies to the people they are about to represent. I want to see a free expression of public opinion here, not a dictatorial sort of declaration that we are a willing host."[20]

Nobody expected Mavrinac to take Ramsay's challenge lying down. But his decision to use Rob Power to threaten Ramsay with a lawsuit was another sign of how poisonous the fight had become.[21] The libel threat not only insisted on a letter of apology, but it also stipulated that Ramsay publicly recant on the need for a referendum. Ramsay was told he must publish his retraction on the referendum in *The Globe and Mail*, *The Toronto Star*, and *The Toronto Sun*.

Ramsay went public, denouncing the letter as "political coercion of the worst kind." He accused the pro–Adams Mine side of trying to "strong-arm" him into "falling into line with the Metro garbage agenda."[22] When pressed by the media about his role in the lawsuit, Power declined comment. "It was our hope that this matter could have been resolved confidentially," he said.

These poisoned fault lines ran right through communities and individual families. The *Northern Daily News* noted the growing bitterness in an August 12, 1995, article: "The entire process has been mired in bad feelings stemming from differences of opinions, not only among the key players but from those who have been neighbors for years."

The fight cut to the heart of the picturesque community of Larder Lake, which had been signed up as a "willing host" community even though it was nearly forty kilometres to the northeast of the Adams Mine. Many in Larder Lake were bothered that nobody had asked them if they wanted to support the garbage. Throughout the summer of 1995, communities in the region had begun holding their own referendums on the project. In Larder Lake, 402 out of 546 people polled said they opposed the project. Only 49 said they supported it.

The *Northern Daily News* said the numbers spoke for themselves. "Nobody can deny the tidal waves of sentiment washing over this whole process. People are damn mad and they're telling anyone and everyone they're not going to take it anymore."[23]

In late September, a group of Larder residents refused to leave a Town Council meeting until the council agreed to send in writing a statement that the community was not a willing host for the project. Losing Larder Lake as a willing host would damage the already troubled process. The dump supporters were determined to make sure this didn't happen. At the next council meeting, pro-dump political supporters were brought in from Kirkland Lake, including members of the Chamber of Commerce, Rob Power, and FACTS member George Duncan. They were backed by uniformed members of the Ontario Provincial Police.[24] Locals found themselves unwanted outsiders at their own council meeting.

Doris Morrison was one of the dump supporters. She ran a local newspaper column entitled "A Proud Daughter of Kirkland Lake." In writing about the people of Larder Lake, she couldn't seem to make up her mind whether they were just "children with temper tantrums" or "eco-terrorists." In her view, it was all about bad manners: "the North has been rude, negative, childlike and hysterical towards a project which could help the economy, and improve health conditions."[25]

Local resident Tracy Boulay had a very different interpretation of what transpired that night. In a letter to the local paper, she wrote that the council relied on outside dump supporters, backed by police, to prevent residents from getting a chance to speak. Local residents who opposed the project were called "uninformed idiots" and told to "sit down and shut up."[26]

"The dissent that is happening in our community will become frightening. I have never encountered such anger and animosity. It's a sad state of affairs when residents of Timiskaming are issued gag orders just because they oppose this project."

These crude attempts to shut down opposition, however, only served to stiffen the growing resistance across the region. Residents began posting homemade signs on their front lawns declaring their unwillingness to accept garbage. Dr. Doug Greenfield was a key leader in organizing people in Larder Lake, while residents Danuta Livingston and Hazel Veinot in Larder Lake went door-to-door to build support from their neighbours.

Throughout the rural towns of Timiskaming, similar local cells of resistance sprang up. Karen Pilch and Sue Wozny organized a team through Chamberlain Township. In Ingram Township, Linda Gauvreau and Mel Booth, along with Jackie and Phyllis Ball, organized the hardscrabble farm families into a force to be reckoned with at regional PLC meetings.

As the public liaison process lumbered on, residents were becoming educated in the issues and increasingly militant in their response. The numerous town hall meetings that filled the calendar through the summer and fall of 1995 laid the groundwork for eventual mass public actions of resistance.

Paying the Piper

Throughout the summer and fall of 1995, the Public Liaison Committee process moved forward under the watchful eyes of hostile public galleries. The PLC was tasked with reviewing the huge stack of consultant reports supplied by Notre Development in advance of a final submission to the provincial Environmental Assessment Board. Many locals felt from the get-go that the fix was in. The promoter was paying the consultants and, not surprisingly, they were all supportive.

The premise was based on twelve test holes that had been drilled at the site in late 1990 by consultant company Golder Associates.[27] The drill holes, none of which reached near the bottom of the pit, were meant to gauge water pressure in the surrounding rock. On a property as large

Opposition among the farmers became increasingly militant as the public process carried on.

and fractured as the Adams Mine, these holes were little more than pin-pricks into the hard, inscrutable back of the Canadian Shield.

The obvious weakness with South Pit was its lack of natural barriers to the water table. This was noted in the first field studies, where the consultants recognized the dangers of contaminants flowing out through fractures at "greater velocities which would be difficult to locate and monitor."[28] The consultant team of Golder Associates turned this problem on its head. They posited that if there was sufficient inward water pressure, the mine could be operated as a giant sump. This theory of "hydraulic containment" was based on the premise that as long as water was being drawn into the pit by a massive pumping system, leachate would not flow out. Hydraulic containment had been used in certain circumstances, but never on a site like the Adams Mine. The depth of the pit, the fractured rock walls, and the inability to accurately predict water flow created numerous unknowns. Nonetheless, the consultants used readings from the twelve drill holes to extrapolate a two-dimensional computer model that promoted the Adams Mine as a reasonable option.

A million litres of groundwater a day were pouring in along the pit walls. Under the Notre plan, this groundwater would be used to carry the contaminated leachate into a massive pumping system, which would push the contaminated groundwater up the equivalent of a sixty-storey building to a water treatment centre. Details of how this treatment plan would treat the roughly sixty thousand chemicals in the contaminated stream were sketchy. But the plant was expected to pump 300 million plus litres a year for the next hundred years into the nearby Misema River. Even if everything went according to plan, the treated water would still contain disturbingly high levels of cadmium, lead, mercury, and vinyl chloride. The flow of contaminants would then make its way down to Lake Timiskaming. No study had been done on the impacts of such long-term contamination.[29]

Running the pumps for a hundred years was based on an arbitrary figure. The contaminating life of garbage is pegged at a thousand years, but the promoters clearly couldn't run pumps for a millennium after they quit town. The way Notre explained it, the dump was scheduled to last just twenty years. For the following eighty years, the pumps would work full out carrying off the worst of the contaminants.[30] What happened once the pumps were turned off was anyone's guess.

Nonetheless, the promoters constructed a computer model that purported to show that, once the pit was full, the leachate would obediently stay within the gravel buffer that separated the waste from the fractured rock walls. This leachate would steadily rise until it reached a level in the pit (325 metres above sea level) where it would flow into an artificial tunnel known as a gravity drainage blanket. This drainage system would have to be monitored, maintained, and pumped for nine more centuries.

Nothing like this had ever been attempted in the landfill business. The depth of the pit would create enormous outward pressure as garbage was piled on over six hundred feet above the base of the pit, which would have no liner. It was all based on the premise that the behaviour of leachate in a fractured pit could be estimated for the coming millennium. In fact, Notre promised to have money in place to deal with any potential environmental problem hundreds of years into the future. They pegged the hourly wages of those pumping the site six hundred years into the future at $25 an hour. To opponents, it seemed the stuff of science fiction, but the Ministry of Environment quickly signed off.

The daunting task of debunking these claims fell to the locals who had been elected to the PLC. This is why PLC members like Joe Muething and Elizabeth Denton fought to level the playing field. The first step was electing a truly independent chair. In the face of opposition from Metro, Notre, and Rob Power, they voted to hire Ron Yurick of Chapleau, Ontario. Yurick was diligent in his job of ensuring scrutiny of all the claims being made by the promoter. It wasn't long before lawyer Power was threatening Yurick about his "attempts to delay or interfere" with the process.[31]

Gordon McGuinty also accused Yurick of fostering a "negative bias" to the project. Yurick's response to McGuinty was revealing:

How does a Chair provide a "negative bias to the project" simply by letting area residents ask questions, particularly when the whole role of the PLC is to provide a forum for local people to pose their difficult questions and have them answered by competent, reasoned responses worked out through scientific inquiry? Is it possible that maybe it's the people themselves who have a "negative bias" toward what the proponent is trying to develop?[32]

Having established an independent chair, the PLC members opposed to the dump were determined to obtain independent advice. The search for a credible independent consultant fell to Muething. Originally from South Florida, Muething had lost his American cadence, but he spoke in the slow, reflective voice of the old South. Muething and his wife, Kathy Martin, relied on the fledgling internet—which played a huge role in levelling the playing field for research and information—to search out independent experts who could help the process. They came across an expert in landfill design known across North America, G. Fred Lee, in El Macero, California. Dr. Lee had also written extensively about the failure of consultants to represent the public interest: "The fact is that consultants do lose business and clients, and opportunities for future work from both government agency and private clients when they do not bend to unjustified inclinations of the client—when they do not say 'what the client wants to hear.'"[33]

Lee felt that one of the reasons for the rise in NIMBYism was that the public had lost faith in so-called experts who are willing to "play the game" of providing the reports that support the position of those who are writing the cheque. Writes Lee:

> The realities of maintaining a client, securing future work, and holding and advancing one's position in a firm, along with inadequate funding to conduct quality and necessary work compel some [engineers/scientists] to exaggerate, diminish or otherwise manipulate the whole truth—despite the fact that codes of ethics . : . emphasize the importance of full disclosure on matters of public health and safety.[34]

In July 1995, Muething, along with PLC members Martha McSherry and Elizabeth Denton, advised the PLC to hire Lee. Not surprisingly, Robert Power opposed the move. He suggested the committee was "throwing away good money."

Nine members voted to hire Lee, while the six who supported the dump proposal voted against. Despite the vote, Metro's overseers refused to allow Lee to be hired. At this point, the Adams Mine opponents took their fight to Toronto. They contacted Councillor Jack Layton, who raised the issue publicly. Feeling the heat, Toronto politicians ordered the Metro

Jack Layton speaking with former Adams miner George McGuire and local volunteers Fran Patterson and Dennis Hakola. Earlton Arena, 2000.

Works team to make the money available to hire Lee and his Canadian assistant, Brian Gallagher.

When Lee joined the peer review team, he made it clear that he was not opposed to the concept of using hydraulic containment at the Adams Mine. His job was to ensure that if the project did go ahead, it was done safely.[35] There were numerous shortcomings with the plan. For example, there was no contingency planning for onsite generators if the power to the landfill gas monitoring system cut out. There were few monitoring wells to track leachate that might escape through the many fissures and cracks.

As the process wore on, Lee became increasingly alarmed at the cavalier response of Metro's planners to such issues. At a presentation to Metro Council in December 1995, he warned councillors that safety was being compromised because the process was being rushed ahead with many major questions left unanswered. He stated that the cost of developing the site safely was radically higher than the picture being presented to Metro Council. Lee estimated that the real cost was at least $1.3 billion higher than the existing price tag of $2 billion—clearly a price that no city would be willing to pay.

Lee's final words on the viability of the mine were much more ominous: "We recommend the public vigorously oppose the approach being taken by Notre Development to the development of this landfill as insufficient to protect the community's interests."[36]

Hold It—Whoops!

By December 1995, the detailed work of the Public Liaison Committee was far from complete. It was, however, becoming apparent that ready or not, it just didn't matter. What mattered was the upcoming vote at Metro Council to sign a new garbage contract. PLC member Joe Muething told Timiskaming media he was frustrated that the political timetable of the city was deemed more important than determining if the site was safe. "Right now we are very rushed. It doesn't give us enough time to complete our work."[37]

One of the key issues was the implication of a "super bore hole" test that Metro had agreed to undertake as a result of growing pressure from the PLC. None of the original drill holes had approached the bottom of the pit, where the outward pressure of leachate would be greatest. Reluctantly Metro Toronto agreed to pay $200,000 for a super bore hole to obtain water pressure readings down to the very bottom of the pit. Twenty-six readings of water flow were taken along the length of the drill hole. Twenty-five of those readings indicated a strong inflow of water that substantiated the proposition of the model.

However, one reading (drill hole DH-95-12) indicated very low water pressure. The proponents dismissed this reading as an "anomaly." Opponents, however, pointed out that if inward water pressure was inconsistent, leachate could easily push outwards into surrounding fractures. This low-pressure reading—the interpretation of which would later become a centrepiece in determining whether the project was legitimate—could indicate that hydraulic containment at the site wasn't possible.

At this time, however, the implications of the reading were overshadowed as the fight moved back to Toronto City Hall. As Notre was pushing to close the deal with Toronto, opponents of the Adams Mine project—with the original grassroots groups TEAC, Northwatch, and REEPA now working together as the Adams Mine Coalition (AMC)—also turned their attention to the political battle in Toronto.

Although I was working as an independent journalist in the north, I began working with the Coalition to help coordinate their media outreach campaign. Provincial media coverage tended to look at the issue through the prism of jobs versus environment. The "human interest" element of such coverage always seemed to tell the story of how the Adams Mine was tearing the region apart, with a pro-job voice countering an anti-dump voice. While such coverage was generally sympathetic to our side, it did little to move the yardstick of provincial public opinion.

We wanted to move the focus of the story to the backroom connections between the dump promoters and Premier Harris. As I began to map out press releases and messaging, we started reaching out to key media to provide them the background story. Toronto's indie magazine *Now* also played an important role. Its article, subtitled "The Road to Garbage Hell Is Paved with Tory Connections," looked into the "scheme to dump on Kirkland Lake."[38] John Barber of *The Globe and Mail* gave us excellent coverage and raised the issue that the north was being targeted because it was seen as a political have-not:

Wanted: garbage pickers. No experience necessary. An exciting opportunity for self-starters with strong stomachs and no hope. . . . If nothing else, the Adams Mine scheme conveys a strong economic and cultural message, "Just because we clawed up all your gold and packed it into vaults on Bay Street, don't think we've forgotten about you. We're going to keep you going by feeding you our predigested leftovers."[39]

These articles helped anchor the media interest in the growing grassroots resistance in Timiskaming.

As Toronto moved to a late-December vote on the Adams Mine, Notre Development knew that the anti-dump message was being heard loud and clear in the city. They decided to mimic our tactic of bringing northern voices to the council table. Notre put together a team of northern politicians and cheerleaders to sing the praises of the dump. Gordon McGuinty worked with every one of them to ensure that their message was consistent with Notre's. For their efforts, they were given free transportation on the Ontario Northlander train.

This cheerleading section was easily drowned out by the rural folk deeply opposed to the plan. These voices weren't given free accommodation on the Northlander. They had to settle for a school bus that left Timiskaming in -45° temperatures at five in the morning. People from communities like Round Lake, Charlton, Hilliardton, and McGarry brought council resolutions and referendums showing the extent of the opposition. Charlton resident Sandra Mitchell was one of the first people on the bus. She was fifty-seventh of ninety-eight people scheduled to speak in the council chambers, and she wasn't given her spot until seven in the evening.

"You would have been proud of your neighbours," Mitchell wrote in a colourful letter to the *Northern Daily News.* "Metro Councillors were quite surprised how vocal, insistent and informed this group was."

The high point of the long day was a homemade model that Ambrose Raftis and New Liskeard high school teacher Doug Fraser presented to the councillors. It was a see-through plastic model of a pit filled with water. As coloured dye (representing leachate) was added to the model, it began leaking out through a crack onto the table and on down onto the carpeted floor. McGuinty's consultants were beside themselves. Frustrated councillor Joan King turned to the consultants and asked why, after the hundreds of thousands spent by the city, the proponents hadn't been able to come up with a three-dimensional model that showed how the pit didn't leak.

In her recap to the local press, Mitchell wrote: "If that wasn't bad enough, McGuinty's engineers asked if they could borrow the opponent's model. Nerve eh? What were they going to do, plug the fault lines with bubble gum?"

The dye left a stain on the council floor. But the model fiasco wasn't the worst of Notre's problems. Many on Metro Council wanted out of the business of running dumps. The hassles of dealing with the north had given many councillors the desire to turn the issue of handling the export of waste over to the private sector. As well, both the Finance and the Environment committees of Metro Council were advising the city to walk on the Adams Mine. Notre's position was becoming increasingly precarious. And when Councillor Jack Layton released details on the true costs of getting the project up and running, the project went into a tailspin.

Throughout the days of public debate, Layton had been pushing for the costs of the project to be made public. On December 13 he was told that the financial data was being "kept secret in the Council clerk's office."[40] The reality was that the data was available; it's just that none of the councillors had actually asked to look at the numbers. But Layton took the time to carefully go through the budget. During the crucial December 19 meeting of council, he confronted council chair Alan Tonks with the fact that project was going to cost $500 million more than what had been claimed. Caught out in the media glare, Tonks scrambled as quickly as he could away from the project he had been staunchly promoting.

"Those figures were a revelation to me. I didn't think they were in the order of that magnitude and all of a sudden you have to say, 'Hold it, whoops.'"[41]

And with that most ignominious of all capitulations—*hold it, whoops*—the Adams Mine plan came crashing down. *The Toronto Star* says the failure of council to undertake basic due diligence left the city looking ridiculous:

> It appears one of the reasons behind the 180 degree turn was that Metro Council simply did not do its homework. Most councillors hadn't bothered to read the detailed reports showing the capital costs of starting up the mine would be $500 million. Council was so single-minded about pursuing the mine project they hadn't seriously considered alternatives such as waste diversion and backyard composting.[42]

It was a classic Layton move. Not only did he hit Tonks hard with numbers that no one else had looked at, but he offered him a face-saving way out by signing on to Layton's less expensive waste diversion deal. "That Layton," said Tonks. "I hate to give it to him but he stimulated us into looking more closely at waste diversion."[43]

The city signed a five-year deal with Republic Services to ship some waste to Michigan while maintaining the Keele Valley site as they prepared a more aggressive waste diversion plan. The Adams Mine proposal appeared dead, but nobody in Timiskaming thought this was the end. As Ambrose Raftis said as the vote went down, "We are pleased to have this victory, but the battle isn't over."

3

Done Deal
1996–1999

It's a done deal. Waste management insiders say that unless
something drastic happens at the Environmental Assessment
hearings being held this month, the plan to build a mega-dump
in Northern Ontario will sail through the approvals process
like a groupie with a backstage pass.

— BRIT GRIFFIN, "Done Deal, The Adams Mine Dump
and the Harris EA," *HighGrader Magazine*, March 1998

You don't have an old iron mine. You have a gold mine of
opportunity. People will be awed by the spectacle of garbage
but also educated by it. We all create garbage but Kirkland Lake,
by becoming the garbage capital of the world, can show people
they are doing something. We can disseminate information about
reducing and re-cycling to change behavior patterns.

— Consultant BILL STEER promoting the eco-tourism benefits of
the Adams Mine garbage dump, *HighGrader Magazine*, July 1999

The campaign built on local cultural activities, such as this country square dance held during a public letter-writing organizing drive in New Liskeard.

Looking for a New Dance Partner

NOTRE WAS BACK AT SQUARE ONE. Though the province had reopened the process, the company had lost the Toronto contract. They had no money. But they still owned a very large hole in the ground, and they had the backing of a militant premier with a majority government.

The first obstacle to getting back on course was dealing with their increasingly uncooperative partner Browning-Ferris Industries. Relations with BFI had never been easy. As a company with $9.1 billion in assets, BFI didn't need to spend much effort keeping Notre happy. They had bought in on the deal with $500,000 cash but, once they had a chance to look at the Adams Mine up close, they were less than impressed.

HighGrader Magazine tracked down Hugh Dillingham, chief landfill engineer for BFI, and got him to speak on the record. He told us that he had come from Dallas to look at the site but quickly realized the plan was contingent on too many unknowns to guarantee a safe and profitable operation. "We decided it would be too expensive to operate [the Adams Mine] with the necessary environmental controls we would have to put in, primarily because of the groundwater infiltration. We looked at the site and decided that the feasibility wasn't there as a result of the technical challenges."[1]

Notre claimed they could operate an unproven pump and flush system for a thousand years into the future. BFI didn't buy it. "We felt that what we would have to install by way of groundwater removal systems would be a) too expensive to support a profitable endeavor and b) it would create challenges down the line from a maintenance point of view," Dillingham explained.

With the Toronto contract lost, Notre was desperate to stay in the game by bidding on some of the contracts in the suburban regions surrounding Toronto. This is where they started to rub BFI the wrong way. BFI had existing landfills in Michigan and also wanted a piece of the Toronto action. As far as BFI was concerned, it was time to cut Notre loose. At a showdown at BFI's head office on Burnhamthorpe Road in Etobicoke, McGuinty almost came to blows with BFI Canadian vice-president Bob Wolfram.[2]

BFI asked for its $500,000 cash back. McGuinty refused. The money had been spent pitching the deal, and now Notre was running on fumes. So BFI walked. After dumping Notre, the company would snag a $65 million piece of the Toronto contract, with a five-year deal to ship waste to one of its Michigan landfills.

The BFI contract and the much larger Republic contract were only short-term. McGuinty says he was told by Premier Harris to bide his time.

It was a day or so before Christmas [1996] and Michael [McGuinty] and
I were having lunch in Valenti's . . . in North Bay. Premier Mike Harris
walked in, saw me and came over to my table. We briefly discussed the
BFI contract, and Mike told me not to worry. Alan Tonks [Metro Council
chair] had come to see him and promised that the U.S. contract would
only be short-term and Toronto would find an Ontario solution; the
Adams Mine would be fine.[3]

To get back in the game, Gordon McGuinty needed a new partner
with deep pockets. This is where Blake Wallace, another Mike Harris
confidant from North Bay, stepped in. According to McGuinty, Wallace
was "well connected to the Ontario Conservative party. He had called
to . . . offer me assistance if I ever needed it."[4]

Busted flush, McGuinty reached out to Wallace, who set up a series
of meetings to find new partners. BFI may have been the second-biggest
waste company in the world, but Wallace set his sights on the largest
one—Waste Management, Inc. The deal with WMI (through its Canadian
subsidiary Canadian Waste Services, or CWS) included an initial pay-
ment to Notre of $350,000 followed by monthly advances of $116,000
for the next two years.[5] They then brought Ontario waste powerhouse
Miller Group, as well as CN, to the table. These companies came together
under the banner of Rail Cycle North (RCN). The next hurdle was getting
approval for the site from the Ministry of Environment (MOE).

Scoping the EA

As 1997 dawned, Gordon McGuinty was feeling so confident he didn't
think it was necessary to submit his plan to an environmental assessment
hearing. From the beginning, the promise of a full and rigorous environmental assessment had been one of Notre's key islands of truth. It was
an island promoted by Kirkland Lake Council since 1990. It was a promise

reiterated by Rob Power at the very first meeting back in 1995, when sceptical local residents had been told that the Adams Mine would undergo the
"most exhaustive review in North America and probably the world."[6]

That was then. This was now. With Mike Harris in power, the regulatory landscape of Ontario had been turned upside down. One of the
key focuses of the Common Sense wrecking crew was Ontario's Ministry
of Environment. Harris was determined to strip the regulatory approvals
process as a way of "opening Ontario up for business." The major project
on the MOE books was the Adams Mine. Harris brought in a series of
changes to the review process that moved the Adams Mine from being a
long shot to an inside favourite almost overnight.

Harris began by axing intervenor funding to citizens' groups that
wished to participate in an EA review. Intervenor funding helped level the
playing field between well-financed waste companies and frustrated local
citizens who lacked the ability to hire independent researchers. Without
intervenor funding, northerners had no means to mount a credible cri-
tique of Notre's high-paid consultants. If they wanted to stand a chance at
the hearing, they had to either come up with their own homemade technical reports, or beg the proponents for financial support.

Harris also empowered the environment minister to decide whether a
project was even entitled to a public hearing. And, if the project was subject to a review, the minister could set limits on how many days of hearings were required and what kind of questions could be asked.

Harris was following a blueprint that had been put together long
before the election of June 1995. While in opposition, he had assembled
a team of advisers to target the cuts and rewrite the rules. The waste policy meetings were chaired by Harris's lieutenant John Snobolen. It was
at one of these meetings in 1994 that Gordon McGuinty first met Rob
Power, and they hit it off immediately.[7]

Harris placed Power on two key advisory committees. Power was
named to the advisory panel to the Environmental Assessment Branch.
He was also picked as the co-chair of a closed-door Policy Advisory

Committee (PAC) that made direct recommendations to both the Conservative Party and to the environment minister.[8]

What was Power's role in rewriting the Environmental Assessment Act? It will never be known, because the ad hoc political committees were exempt from Access to Information provisions. When pressed by *Now* magazine in 1998, Power stated, "I had nothing to do with the rewriting of the EA Act."[9]

But Gordon McGuinty tells a different story. "Yes, during the Harris term his [Power's] advice was sought on legislative changes, and yes, he had access to the inner workings of the Conservative government. I refuse to apologize for that. . . . Was Rob consulted on changes to the *Environmental Assessment Act*? He definitely was."[10]

Little wonder that McGuinty didn't think it was necessary to slow the project down by submitting it to a public review. Power, however, felt differently. He reminded McGuinty of the public's belief that this was a deal between two North Bay golfing buddies. For the sake of political perception, Power suggested they agree to a hearing.

Rob Power was wearing many hats. He had provided input to Harris on rewriting the regulatory landscape. He had helped steer the Public Liaison Committee and worked with McGuinty to negotiate the political agenda at the provincial level. Now, as the lawyer for Notre Development, he was going to be the first lawyer to test the new rules of environmental assessment.

For tactical reasons, Notre Development limited its application to the South Pit; there were too many problems with selling hydraulic containment at all three large pits, and the track record for expanding operating landfill sites meant eventually expansion would likely not be difficult. Under the plan submitted to the Ministry of Environment, Notre asked for an initial licence to deal with 20 million tonnes of waste (as compared to the 40 to 60 million tonnes originally planned).[11]

But even then, the project faced major stumbling blocks. For example, one of the key questions was Rail Cycle North's ability to run the

Timiskaming residents on the move. Opposition was centred on the threat to the groundwater supply of the region. March for Water rally, July 2000. PHOTO: courtesy of Kathy Hakola

pumping system for a century after the dump closed and then maintain monitoring of the site for the coming thousand years.

HighGrader Magazine ran the proposition past Henk Haitjema, an international expert in groundwater modelling at the School of Public and Environmental Affairs in Bloomington, Indiana. He couldn't even begin to get his head around the claim. The depth of the pit and the sheer volume of water created numerous unpredictables. "It is quite a proposal to pump for 100 years. Look at the energy expense. It's one thing to put a landfill in a couple of feet beneath the groundwater table, but it's quite another to have to pump massive amounts of ground water to create a negative gradient."[12]

Dr. Haitjema pointed out that if the pumps cut out and the pit flooded, the premise immediately fell apart. But these questions weren't going to be asked at the environmental assessment review. Thanks to the changes brought in by Harris, the Adams Mine was not going to be subject to a full review. Instead, the minister decided to "scope" the terms of what would be studied. The Adams Mine review was limited to a mere thirteen days (EA hearings usually took more than six months). The MOE also instructed the panel to limit its investigation to one question—whether or not the two-dimensional computer model that predicted hydraulic containment at the site was reasonable.

Ambrose Raftis accused the MOE of acting as an extension of the promoter: "What was scoped out of it [the EA] was the areas where the project will fail. It's an experimental site. Nobody knows whether it's going to work or not. The way the hearing has been set up leaves much of the responsibility for proof to the public. We don't have the money to do that."[13]

Under the Harris government, the EA process had become politicized and arbitrary. In an essay written in 1999, legal researchers Mark Winfield and Paul Muldoon were scathing in their assessment of the impacts of the Common Sense Revolution on environmental protection:

> [We] have witnessed an unprecedented dismantling of the mechanisms for ensuring the legal and political accountability of the provincial government for the decisions that it makes about Ontario's environment and natural resources. . . . These measures not only threaten the protection of the province's environment, they also present a challenge to the basic principles of parliamentary democracy, responsible government and the rule of law.[14]

The Environmental Assessment Hearing

Even with the odds lined up against them, Adams Mine opponents were convinced the site had enough problems to sink the project. The Coalition had been in touch with hydrogeologist Paul Bowen. He felt there were many problems with the plan, including the decision not to use a liner in the pit. This was a decision that "was driven by purely economic concerns. Not having a liner means there is no margin of error—if hydraulic containment fails, there is nothing to prevent leachate from moving relatively rapidly off site."[15]

Bowen felt that precedent was on the side of the opposition. He pointed to the recent EA decision to deny a permit to a waste project at the Steetley Quarry in Southern Ontario. Like Adams Mine, Steetley had been promoted on a theoretical hydraulic containment plan prepared by Golder Associates.

Environmental lawyer Rick Lindgren was working with the Coalition. According to Lindgren's notes, Bowen felt that the complex hydrogeology of the Adams Mine coupled with the lack of actual data would make it difficult for the ministry to ignore the ruling they had rendered in the Steetley case: "There is an alarming paucity of detailed design information. Most of the material is still largely at the conceptual level. . . . the same consultants [Golder] provided a much greater level of detail/design drawings in Steetley [and still got rejected by the Board]."[16]

But the Steetley project hadn't been a pet project of the Common Sense revolutionaries. Ministry of Environment bureaucrats were blunt with Bowen. "The Adams Mine [review] will not be Steetley II."[17]

In laying down the ground rules for the hearing, the Ministry of Environment removed many problematic areas for the Notre team. One of those problematic areas was the outstanding land interests of Timiskaming First Nation (TFN). Although the reserve was based in Notre Dame du Nord, Quebec (twenty-six kilometres from New Liskeard), their traditional territory encompassed the region that would be impacted by millions of litres of treated leachate being pumped into the Misema and Blanche Rivers. Timiskaming First Nation had made their concerns known to the promoter, Metro, and the province. They had been blown off. Premier Harris had already established himself as no friend to Aboriginal land claims. He certainly wasn't going to welcome a claim from a Quebec band. Thus the issue of Aboriginal rights and impacts were simply scoped out of the review—a decision that would come to haunt the promoters in the years to come.

John Vanthof says it was clear the outcome was already decided. "I was told by a high-placed Conservative cabinet minister that we were wasting our breath. This project had been given the gold star. Nobody in the industry or the ministry was going to put their jobs on the line speaking out against this plan."

In preparation for the environmental assessment, the northern opposition came together under the name Adams Mine Intervention Coalition (AMIC). Local groups REEPA and TEAC had already begun to coalesce as the Adams Mine Coalition. They were joined for the purposes of the EA by the Temiskaming Federation of Agriculture. Brennain Lloyd of the North Bay–based environmental group Northwatch played a key role in coordinating the various organizations and advisers under this new umbrella organization. Joe Muething and Ambrose Raftis helped prepare questions for the team. Environmental lawyer Rick Lindgren represented the group.

From the beginning, Vanthof felt that the lack of independently funded consultants and lawyers doomed the process. This was a play-for-keeps venue, and yet Lindgren advised his clients that the EA hearing should not be considered an adversarial courtroom drama. Rob Power, representing the other side, didn't believe such codswallop for a moment. He was there to win. The Notre witnesses went through practice sessions where they finessed their arguments and rehearsed their responses.

The two sides faced off against each other on March 23, 1998, before a three-person panel chaired by Len Gertler, professor emeritus of the University of Waterloo. He was joined by political appointee Pauline Browes (a recently defeated Conservative MP) and Thunder Bay city councillor Don Smith.

The marching season. Rallies and marches were used to build confidence in the public to participate in non-violent actions. July 2000.

In many ways, the hearing became a battle of highly paid experts versus local amateurs. The amateurs had done extensive work to debunk the infallibility of a hypothetical model by pointing to the reality of what happens over time with the interaction of garbage, rock, and water. But Notre's team of geologists and engineers kept the message simple—the pumps will work, the drainage blanket (a gravel sieve surrounding the pit walls) won't clog, the site will maintain hydraulic containment. The model showed it, it must be thus.

When asked what would happen if the gravel blanket began to clog with garbage, Golder engineer Frank Barone didn't blink. "It won't [clog]," he replied.[18] When pressed about the lack of contingency planning in case the pumps failed or the site did not work according to the model, engineer Doug McLachlin told the hearing not to worry. "It's highly unlikely contingency plans would have to be implemented at the site," he said."[19]

The promoters had clearly learned their lesson from the push and shove of the Public Liaison Committee process. They kept their answers short, pithy, and self-assured. Joe Muething says the professionals on the promoters' team simply went around the detailed "what if" questions being raised by the amateur locals. "The problem with the EA," recalls Muething, "is that we were dealing with very complex issues that were being decided on a few key sound bites provided by their experts."

For example, when the issue of maintaining hydraulic containment for a thousand years was put to the Notre team, they countered that there were uranium mines in Saskatchewan that used hydraulic containment to contain radioactive waste for a million years. There were enormous differences between the Rabbit Lake tailings system in Saskatchewan and the proposed Adams Mine plan.[20] Nonetheless, Muething says this claim of a million years' security was enough to win over panellist Pauline Browes. "She was sold right then and there. Never mind that the site in Saskatchewan and the Adams Mine were completely different. . . . It was absurd, but I knew right then and there that we had lost her and she was sold on the project."

Still, despite their carefully thought-out plan, the Notre team was running into trouble. Their biggest problem was presenting a credible case for how to control the flow of leachate for the nine long centuries after the pumps were turned off. Despite the emphatic promises from the hired guns, there was no scientific or technological evidence to explain why the leachate in a waterlogged pit would obediently flow upwards to an artificial exit, rather than simply flowing out into the surrounding fractures.

The discussion kept coming back to the questionable borehole DH-95-12. Strong inward water pressure would be required to prevent the enormous outward pressure on leachate once the pit was full of garbage. And yet, the anomalous reading from 95-12 indicated there could be dangerously low inward pressure at certain points along the pit walls. If the pit leaked, the promise of drawing off leachate into a drainage trench near the surface was little more than a pipe dream.

But Notre's crew stuck to the original talking point—the pits won't leak. "After twenty years of mining, no witness can suggest there is any outward flow of water," stated Rob Power to the nods of the consultants. Never mind that former Adams miners George McGuire and Dave Keith were at the hearing as witnesses to provide first-hand accounts of the water problems in the pits.

The witnesses who brought real-life experience to the hearing were at a disadvantage. These witnesses were attempting to point out the numerous problems that would occur with an experimental site over a long period of time. The Notre consultants, however, only had to prop up the soundness of a computer model. The witnesses with the credentials at the end of their names simply counted for more.[21]

As Joe Muething concludes, "Notre had the attitude that, since they had spent millions on the project, therefore it must be safe."

The one chance for a level playing field between the consultants and the northern opposition came when the experts from the Ministry of Environment came forward. The MOE team included ministry lawyer Pat Moran, provincial hydrogeologist Ernst Zaltsberg, and senior engineer David Staseff. But if anyone thought that MOE would play the role of good cop, it was time to think again.

Dr. Zaltsberg gave the project the thumbs-up. "Hydraulic containment is feasible and viable . . . [the plan has] been clearly confirmed by modelling results."[22] Staseff concurred. "The proposed hydraulic containment design is an effective solution for containment and collection of leachate generated at the site."

AMIC lawyer Rick Lindgren tried to refocus the panel on the fundamental uncertainty of the site. "Twenty years of profit, a thousand years of potential liability and environmental impact. Quite frankly, Mr.

Chairman, this is not a legacy the board should approve on the evidence or on principle."

But once again, the MOE cheerfully stood by Notre. "It's a simple design, very easy to understand and easy to make a determination on whether it's feasible," said ministry lawyer Moran. He suggested that any problems could be ironed out as they drafted the conditions of approval for the site. Problem solved.

At the end of the MOE's closing arguments, Joe Muething remembers how miner George McGuire blew up at Moran. "You son of a bitch," he said. "I thought you were there to protect the public. You acted like a goddamned salesman for McGuinty."

The way Muething remembers it, the MOE staffers attempted to smooth things over by offering the opposition a deal that seemed too good to refuse. Once Notre was given its Certificate of Approval for the site (as if this was already a given), the Ministry of Environment would allow the members of the Adams Mine Intervention Coalition to write the terms and conditions that Notre needed to abide by in order to operate the dump.

But AMIC wasn't impressed. According to Muething, Moran was dumbfounded at their refusal. This offer would ensure citizen oversight. It was like being given a blank cheque, he told them. "Big deal," Muething responded. "Everybody knows the cheque will bounce."

The Adams Mine volunteers knew that once a dump site has been approved for taking waste, the terms and conditions could easily be ignored, bypassed, or rewritten. "Sure, we could have written anything we wanted onto those terms and conditions. None of it would have meant anything. Once the pit was up and running, the MOE could change it or ignore our conditions and in exchange they would have bought our support."

Muething says the MOE team was at a loss. "This was how they thought the game was played. They would bring us into the process, and everybody gets to go home happy. But we didn't come to play the game."

Rubber Stamp in a Back Room

Just as the MOE lawyers had predicted, Notre received approval from the Environmental Assessment Board, along with a long list of conditions. But it was hardly a ringing endorsement. On June 19, 1998, the panellists released a one-page statement announcing that the project was being approved by a split decision. Len Gertler and Pauline Browes had given their support, while Don Smith dissented over the uncertainty of the hydraulic containment system and the thousand years of maintenance required. But the board had agreed to twenty-six conditions that must be met prior to the project going into operation.

One of the key requirements under the Certificate of Approval was to drill two further deep boreholes under the pit to determine whether the low water readings in DH-95-12 were an anomaly or indicative of underlying trouble. The cost of these two new holes was $300,000. The problem was, now that Notre had a Certificate of Approval, who would assess the results of the drilling? The EA Board punted the responsibility back to the Ministry of Environment. This was a real source of concern for the Adams Mine opposition, who believed the ministry tended to act like an extension of Notre. Brennain Lloyd of Northwatch said the MOE couldn't be trusted. "I'm very disappointed the board handed over their responsibility to an MOE bureaucrat who is unidentified and inaccessible."[23]

In November 1998, two drill holes, DH-98-1 and 98-2, were undertaken. When the results of these tests were examined, they contradicted the predictions on which the model was based. Rather than showing strong upward water pressure, the drills hit numerous places of exceedingly low water pressure. This meant that unless the pumps were kept running in perpetuity to maintain inward pressure, the gravity drainage phase was simply not possible.

The Ministry of Environment had a problem on its hands. The EA had been limited to the question of whether or not the computer model was credible. Under the terms and conditions of the Environmental

Assessment, the MOE was not supposed to issue final approval unless it could state "without reservation" that the field tests confirmed the model. The field tests had just done the opposite.

But in Mike Harris's Ontario, ministry bureaucrats weren't about to rock the boat. They told Golder to create a new model to explain away the difficult new field data. The beauty of a computer model is that, provided you tinker long enough with the inputs, it will give you whatever result you want.

Golder invoked a supposition that allowed the computer to assume that as garbage filled the pit, water levels in the surrounding rock would rise as well. Presto, according to the new model, there was no longer any problem. This revised model was presented to MOE officials behind closed doors without any public review.

Dr. Zaltsberg, who had given the thumbs-up to the hydraulic containment theory during the Environmental Assessment Hearing, now had the responsibility of reviewing Golder's rewrite. In a memo to MOE senior engineer David Staseff, he warned that the model could not be verified by any real-life data:

> It is necessary to point out that this confirmation [of hydraulic containment] is derived exclusively from the modelling results. The model applied is based on several assumptions which cannot be verified in the field. The hypothetical nature of many assumptions and the inability to verify them in the field cause inevitable uncertainty associated with the range of expected groundwater level rebound during the gravity drainage phase.[24]

Thus, behind closed doors, key ministry staff were saying the same thing that the people of Timiskaming had been saying all along. "The hypothetical nature" of the entire project would cause "inevitable uncertainty" as to its safety. The most controversial dump plan in Canadian history had been approved based on a model that couldn't be proven. If ministry staff had expressed reservations publicly, the project would have been blown out of the water. And yet, the Ministry of Environment allowed the proponents to simply replace their failed model with one that was unverifiable. Everything was back on track, and Zaltsberg's less-than-positive memo wasn't made public.

The Adams Mine Intervention Coalition attempted to challenge the decision in court, but the judge didn't give them the time of day. After all, the Ministry of Environment had reviewed the project. What more was there to say? Notre was on its way.

As for Robert Power, Premier Harris gave him a plum patronage appointment as the chair of the provincial Trillium Foundation.

Gordon McGuinty was over the moon. "The war on whether this project will go ahead is all over," he said. "Placards or pickets won't hold up the project."[25] The stage was set for the inevitable moment when McGuinty would have to put his boast to the test.

4

Dropping the Gloves
May–August 2000

Our people are tired of the runaround. They've reached
the end of being nice guys. And they're going to do
whatever it takes in order to protect their area.
— JOHN NYCHUK, June 2000

This is a dump. It is the ultimate insult of industrial Canada to the
north. What we are fighting for is all of the northern belt—northern
Quebec, northern Manitoba, northern Alberta. We are the first to fall.
If we fall, believe me the other open pit mines and sites will fall
because this is too easy for Southern Ontario.
— PIERRE BELANGER, CBC national television, October 2000

The Lines Are Drawn

HAVING SECURED the Certificate of Approval at the Adams Mine,
Notre Development, along with its partners in the Rail Cycle
North consortium, turned their attention to wooing Toronto
City Council. The old Metro Council had disappeared, following the forced
amalgamation of the city boroughs in 1998. A long-term twenty-year

waste contract, to replace the five-year contract with Republic Services in Michigan, was one of the main goals of this new amalgamated council. A deal was expected to be signed by October 2000, just prior to the upcoming civic elections. In addition to the Toronto negotiations, Rail Cycle North was bidding on further contracts in the surrounding GTA communities of York, Durham, and Peel. Opening the dump would be a billion-dollar-plus deal, and Rail Cycle North pulled out all the stops to ensure the deal didn't slip away like it had two times before.

In Toronto, opposition to the plan coalesced around Councillor Jack Layton. He had done enormous damage to Notre's 1990 and 1995 bids. Layton's assistant Franz Hartmann had the task of helping to organize the dozen-plus city councillors who were lining up to fight the project. Layton's office worked closely with the Toronto Environmental Alliance on raising awareness among Torontonians about the negative consequences associated with the Adams Mine option. As well, many grassroots Toronto activists like Dave Meslin and Warren Brubacher kept council's feet to the fire on the issue, promoting progressive recycling and waste diversion strategies.

In the north, the unresolved question was whether the opposition would move beyond grumbling to committed action. As one CBC producer said to me, "You tell me that people will fight this dump, but will this be just another case of Northern Ontario crying itself back to sleep?"

It was a fair comment. Northern Ontario had a long history of complaining about its treatment by the south and yet, all too often, northerners sullenly went along once Queen's Park put its foot down. The region had been very quiet in the year following the positive EA decision. Given the momentum behind Rail Cycle North at Queen's Park and Toronto City Hall, northerners would need to raise a mighty racket to scare city councillors off the Adams Mine express train. As 2000 dawned, it was obvious that there was a very short window of time in which to organize a force to be reckoned with.

The first test came in May 2000 when Layton tipped off local opposition leaders that senior Toronto councillors and staff were set to visit the Adams Mine site. The visit was set for May 26 as part of the Works Committee's due diligence process in the lead-up to signing a contract. As soon as local organizers got wind of the trip, phones across the region started ringing.[1]

The plan was simple enough—get in your car and join the convoy heading to the Adams Mine site. The convoy began in New Liskeard and as it moved along the hundred-kilometre route, cars from various townships joined. As the vehicles turned east on Highway 112, the Timiskaming convoy was joined by cars from Kirkland Lake, Matachewan, and Larder Lake. Together they made their way up the seven-kilometre Adams Mine Road, led by a purple-laced flatbed truck carrying a large, white coffin adorned with the name "Temiskaming."

By mid-morning, the length of the Adams Mine Road was blocked with vehicles. Notre had a huge problem on its hands. If Toronto councillors were going to visit the mine, they would have to run a hostile gauntlet in full view of the media.

Local opposition to the project had long been Notre's Achilles' heel. The dump promoters had assured city officials that when push came to shove, the resistance would crumble, common sense would prevail, and the northern residents would accept their fate.

But Gordon McGuinty was worried. He told local media that if this protest was successful, it could "put a nail in the coffin" of his plan. Rather than risk having Toronto city councillors see the extent of this opposition, he chartered two helicopters to ferry the city officials from the airport to the mine site.

The dump promoters certainly thought they had got the better of the folks stranded along the mine road. But as word spread among the hundreds of protesters that the Toronto councillors had simply flown over them, dissatisfaction rose to anger. This casual contempt for local input had been made manifestly clear during the public consultation and subsequent environmental assessment process. It now felt like the time for pushing back had finally arrived. As nervous police guarded the gates of the mine filming potential troublemakers, some protesters wanted to break through the cordon of police and confront the councillors at the mine.

Hours ticked by. The protesters sat on their car hoods blocking an empty road to a shutdown mine. And then it dawned on them that they weren't the ones who were holding the weak hand.

"What is McGuinty going to do when it comes to getting his garbage past us," one farmer shouted, "fly the garbage in by helicopter? We control this road. We will decide what happens here." The convoy then turned around and headed on the long, winding road to the airport. If city officials wouldn't meet protesters at the mine, they'd have to meet them as they tried to board the plane.

When the helicopters landed at Kirkland Lake airport for the trip home, Notre's crew attempted to hustle the officials onto the plane, but Councillor Jack Layton broke free. He pointed to the crowd of people being held back by the chain-link fence. "These are people from the region," he declared. "And we should go over and see them." There was little the delegation could do but stand there and receive an earful from the protesters.

Notre attempted to downplay the impact of this protest. A local pro-dump editorialist trashed the people who were involved in what turned out to be the first blockade of the Adams Mine Road. "It was a parade complete with clowns and floats . . . the actions of these protesters are threatening to Kirkland Lake and this region. They are standing in the path of progress, keeping jobs away. . . . It's time these protesters pack up their signs, return their tasteless coffins and go home."[2]

The only problem was, these people were home. The May 26 skirmish only added to a growing determination in otherwise mild-mannered country folk. The response of retired resident Hugh Reynolds was typical. He penned an angry letter to Toronto mayor Mel Lastman.

"The first kiss." Farmers shut down rail line at Earlton. June 2, 2000. PHOTO: Darlene Wroe, courtesy of *The Temiskaming Speaker*

Last Friday every possible means was used to avoid your delegation from seeing and hearing for themselves the extent of the opposition. An opposition, not of "environmentalists" but ordinary people. . . . In a shameful act of intimidation, more than 20 OPP cruisers, helicopters and unmarked vehicles were called "to protect" your delegates and to keep the protesters from making contact with them. . . . We are not prepared to tolerate Toronto politicians deciding to dump their city's garbage into what is the largest well in the area.[3]

A little more than two weeks later, the farmers of Timiskaming upped the ante significantly when they committed the first act of civil disobedience by shutting down the Ontario Northland Railway. The farmers organized a two-pronged convoy of tractors and farm equipment, one coming on the tracks from the north and one from the south. They met at the rail crossing in the heart of the village of Earlton.

John Vanthof stepped onto the rail tracks and put the city on notice. "It's not up to Metro Toronto to decide what is going to happen in Northern Ontario. Today is the day we start to protect ourselves," he declared. The people of Timiskaming were not about to cry themselves to sleep. The fight was on.

The First Kiss

Among the quaint boutiques of downtown New Liskeard, a new shop was opening. On a hot summer evening in July 2000, a ribbon-cutting ceremony was held and local people were invited to stop by for a coffee and to meet the volunteer staff. Retired Kirkland Lake schoolteacher Barb Biederman-Bukowski cut the ribbon. She came decked out in a jaunty summer hat and a T-shirt emblazoned "SAY NO TO ADAMS MINE."

Biederman-Bukowski had been watching the fight from the sidelines for years. Now she was one of a crew of new volunteers stepping forward to run the phones and fax machines in the newly opened Adams Mine campaign office. People knew that Rail Cycle North had a full-time team of lobbyists and planners promoting the dump. The local opposition decided to set up its own office and establish a team that could work full out to counter them. The days of part-time, makeshift resistance were over.

Landys Hillman and Linda Miller, two local volunteers, became self-appointed office managers. Miller, from the village of Thornloe, wasn't shy about ordering into action the numerous folk coming through the door looking to help. She kept the office running six days a week. Hillman was equally tenacious doing research and working the phones.

Earlton business owner Pierre Belanger was another volunteer who attended the ribbon-cutting ceremony. Belanger didn't fit the bill of radical. He was an RV salesman, buffalo rancher, regional economic development planner, and player in the local Liberal Party. Just prior to the Adams Mine proposal, Belanger had been part of a group who considered supporting a landfill project for Toronto in the Earlton farm region, but he'd backed out when he realized it would bring little economic benefit and mark the region as a dumping zone.

Belanger was well connected. He made calls to business leaders across the north to help pay for radio and television advertising. He called on friendly Liberal senators in Ottawa to get involved in a federal investigation into the plan. And he also played a major role in building alliances with grassroots organizations in neighbouring Abitibi-Témiscamingue, Quebec.

Belanger brought a calm, bourgeois respectability to the movement, which made him an ideal spokesperson with national media. But he had his own history in protest politics. As a youth, Belanger had cut his teeth fighting for language and cultural rights for rural Franco-Ontarians. He understood how issues of sovereignty and pride could be used as powerful motivating forces. Belanger framed the Adams Mine fight as an issue of northern identity. He inspired local blue-collar folk to see themselves as defending the legacy of the north. They were too proud, too independent, and too fierce to ever bow down as "garbagemen for Toronto."

The clock was ticking with barely three months to the Toronto vote. Throughout the EA process, Notre had been in the driver's seat. Now it was our turn. As a media coordinator for this phase of the battle, I established a three-month calendar. We set the objective of ensuring two media events a week, and planned to use evenings or weekends for organizing rallies and town halls to build the volunteer forces and to increase their comfort with increasingly radical action.

The planning was done on two levels. There was a weekly (sometimes twice-weekly) meeting of an inner planning team of the Adams Mine Coalition that included myself, Terry Graves, Pierre Belanger, Joseph

Gold, Brennain Lloyd, and Ambrose Raftis. The Adams Mine Intervention Coalition of 1998 had reverted back to a less-structured alliance between the local grassroots citizens' groups and the Temiskaming Federation of Agriculture. Nonetheless, the TFA's John Vanthof often sat in on meetings with the AMC planning team as we weighed out various scenarios and tested them for potential strengths and weaknesses. These meetings were like elaborate war-game sessions. With the short timeline ahead of us, we couldn't afford a misstep. Each potential action sought to bring the maximum pressure to bear on the other side's weakest links.

Once a strategy had been worked out, it was brought to the larger weekly "war council" meeting at the Grand Boulevard Restaurant in Earlton. This group brought together various municipal, farm, and volunteer activists around a large U-shaped table in the back of the restaurant. The strategies that had been suggested by the smaller planning team were vetted and either approved, modified, or rejected.

The membership of these planning teams was never set in stone. Various people came in and out throughout the campaign. Each of us brought different skill sets and tactical considerations. I brought my skills as a journalist to the table. On the tactical front, I had always had a fascination with the work of Chicago grassroots organizer Saul Alinsky. The original shit disturber, he built his campaigns around the natural strengths of a community and well-placed pressure points.

Throughout Timiskaming people would gather in church basements, legions, and country halls. It wasn't hard to fill a hall in the long summer days. The best way to build the organization was to utilize the deeply entrenched familial, religious, cultural, and work-related networks. These community links created comfortable paths to move people into action.

One of the first lessons learned was that Sunday afternoon (the time between church and getting set for a family dinner) was an ideal time to hold a public meeting. Among the organizers, we began calling Sunday afternoon gatherings the "garbage church." These meetings were founded on four principles:

1) *Every meeting had to inspire.* We relied on excellent public speakers like Pierre Belanger and retired professor Joseph Gold to galvanize people into fighting for the sovereignty of their region.

2) *Every participant was an organizer.* "Each one reach one, each one teach one" was our slogan: everyone who came to the meetings was given the tools to go out and bring others into the movement.

3) *Every meeting had to raise funds.* We knew we were fighting against a well-oiled corporate machine and regularly made contributions. Rev. Mike Shute had a great line for raising money: "The good news is that we have all the money we need to beat this dump. The only problem is that the money is sitting in your pockets."

4) *Every participant had a task to fulfil.* Rural people are practical and prefer action to words. Meetings that are just bitch sessions will drain their energy. The success of the campaign was based on involving individuals by giving them tasks and targets to ensure their personal participation.

One of the first tasks for building public involvement was a letter-writing campaign. Local organizers set a goal of a thousand letters from the region. (Soon, the letter-writing campaigns would reach the tens of thousands.) They held coffee parties, went door to door, and created public events to encourage potential letter-writers to stick around and sign on to the movement.

In mid-June 2000, a letter-writing day was held at the New Liskeard farmers' market. The Adams Mine Coalition invited square dance groups, children's choirs, and local musicians to provide entertainment. The fiddle sounds of the Blanche River Ramblers shared the stage with the country rock sounds of musicians from Timiskaming First Nation.

Those who stopped in were invited to go over to tables where letters were signed and collected. One of the letter-writing coordinators was Shirley Dorsey, a long-time volunteer at Kirkland Lake Legion Branch 87.

If Shirley asked you to sign a letter, how could you say no? In no time at all, over 3,500 letters had been gathered.

The letter-writing campaigns were having their effect. Notre Development went to the length of taking out a full-page ad warning people not to go to the letter-writing workshops. The advertisement stated:

> TO THE RESIDENTS OF TEMISKAMING—THE FULL STORY: The planned "letter writing campaign" to the City of Toronto will once again be based on misinformation, innuendo and fear mongering. It should not be endorsed by residents of Temiskaming.[4]

Although there was a central organizing committee for larger strategy, the pathways to radicalization were built by decentralized teams who organized their own communities. The big step that dump opponents needed to take was to realize that confrontation and civil disobedience were almost a certainty. For some in this rural region, that was a huge psychological step. During one organizing meeting, a local farmwoman spoke up.

"I am getting very uncomfortable with the direction of this conversation," she admonished. "What you are talking about is civil disobedience. As a Christian woman, I do not support breaking the law."

Pierre Belanger turned to her with sly smile. "Madame, I understand your worries. It's like when you're in high school and you keep thinking about that first kiss. What will it be like? What if I don't do it right? And then it just happens. You have that first kiss and you think, 'Hey, I like this. Let's go further.'"

Harris Forces Toronto's Hand

In its efforts to lock down the Toronto deal, Rail Cycle North sought out political "intelligence" much as it had earlier sought supportive consultants. The intelligence came in the form of Jeffrey S. Lyons, the ultimate lobbyist/power broker at city hall. "Brother Jeff" (as Mayor Lastman called him) was king of the back room. (He would later become *persona non grata* at city hall for his involvement in the 2005 MFP computer contract scandal, but would reappear with the election of Mayor Rob Ford.) McGuinty also had other big players in his corner, such as Paul Godfrey, former Metro chair and now CEO of *The Toronto Sun*.

And yet, Rail Cycle North was learning that you couldn't buy political intelligence with the same assuredness that you can buy reports for an EA. In June 2000, McGuinty was blind-sided by the news that the Toronto Works Committee was about to advise council to drop the Adams Mine option altogether.

The Works Committee warned Toronto against locking itself into the controversial Adams Mine project. Instead, the committee advised that Toronto buy time in order to establish a larger and more aggressive waste diversion strategy. The key to making this happen was diverting 600,000 tonnes of annual commercial waste from Keele Valley, extending the lifespan of the municipal landfill by four years until 2006. The city would pick up the slack with three smaller landfills—Green Lane landfill in London, a site in Essex, and the Onyx landfill in Michigan. This would allow the city to save $65 million and give it time to establish a rigorous waste diversion plan.

Notre Development was once again on the ropes. But the difference from the debacles of 1990 and 1995 is that this time, they had the premier in their corner. Almost immediately, Harris kicked into action. Before anyone had a chance to study the Works report, the premier announced he would block any efforts to keep Keele Valley open.

Toronto Works chair Bill Saundercook accused Harris of political interference. "The Province said it would not micromanage our garbage problem but now they are going to shut Keele and not compensate Toronto for the loss. They are making it very difficult for Toronto to function."[5]

As Rail Cycle North scrambled to deal with the threat posed by an extended life at Keele Valley, their main competitor, Republic Services of Michigan, which was looking to extend the five-year contract it had signed in late 1995, offered the city a cut-rate deal to win the lucrative Toronto contract. "We can take the garbage right away by truck or rail, whatever the Council wants," stated Bob Webb of Republic.[6] Toronto announced it would accept Republic's lower bid and gave Rail Cycle North barely a week to respond. McGuinty called in political favours to get what he needed—a peek at Republic's sealed bid.

In his memoir, McGuinty lays out the issue: "We had a big problem. . . . We needed new political intelligence. And within twenty-four hours, from two separate sources, Republic's price became available to RCN. . . . Fair is fair—and so much for that so-called confidentiality of Toronto Council and their staff."[7]

Armed with inside information about the competitor's bid, Rail Cycle North shaved off $50 million from its own offer in order to stay in the game. Knowing that the project could easily be scuttled at the upcoming Toronto Works Committee meetings of July 20–21, the RCN crew began calling in other political favours.

In the lead-up to the Toronto Works meeting of July, the Adams Mine Coalition staged another show of militancy. The March for Water was designed to force a temporary shutdown of both Highway 11 and the Ontario Northland rail crossing at New Liskeard. The ONR was a key supporter of the Adams Mine project. John Wallace, president of Ontario Northland, issued a stern warning to the marchers: "We will not tolerate any illegal acts which prevent us from conducting our business in a safe, uninterrupted manner. If they [protesters] attempt to trespass on our property, we expect charges to be laid."[8]

If Wallace hoped to scare off participants, he failed. Over six hundred people showed up for the march. When it reached the ONR rail crossing, police made no effort to stop protesters who began to fan out along the tracks.

This shutdown of both the highway and rail line hardly seemed like a confrontation at all. Everyone was friendly and cordial. Retired high school teacher Doug Worth walked the lines of police, shaking hands and thanking them for their excellent service to the community. One of the underlying objectives of this march was to ensure that participants came away feeling invigorated and ready to take the next step. This march was a key field exercise for training a volunteer army of people who were willing to walk, march, and, if necessary, shut down roads.

While the Adams Mine Coalition was working to raise the pressure on the city, the Adams Mine promoters were equally intent on sending councillors a forceful message. Once again, Premier Harris was the man of the hour. The premier had recently reinforced his close relationship with Gordon McGuinty by sending him a personal video greeting to celebrate McGuinty's fiftieth birthday.[9] Now Harris sent an even more important gift.

In the midst of the heated Toronto Council debate on July 21, Harris sent a letter to chair Bill Saundercook confirming his intention to shut the Keele Valley site, effectively torpedoing Toronto's attempt to find a way out of their garbage crisis. The letter was a follow-up to a June 20 letter from Deputy Minister Cameron Clark that reminded Saundercook that "the Adams Mine represents the only complete Ontario based solution . . . the Ministry does not wish to see the Adams Mine site excluded from further consideration on the grounds that there is no endorsement by a 'willing host' community."[10]

Protesters be damned. Harris was adamant: the Adams Mine was going ahead and City Council dutifully complied. Following this interim vote by council to keep moving forward with the Adams Mine negotiations, a group of very glum Toronto activists met with their northern counterparts in a room at Toronto City Hall. The final council vote was now just two months away, and it appeared as if this was a done deal. For city activists like Franz Hartmann, the vote was a devastating example of how big money and backroom deals could sideswipe a progressive alternative.

"I thought it was over," Hartmann recalls. "I had been in politics long enough to know we were up against impossible odds." And yet, Councillor Jack Layton came into the activists' meeting on fire. "We will win this," he urged the group. "Let's not give up."

Layton's leadership at this moment was a turning point in his relationship with the northern organizers. The northern team knew what needed to be done on their end, but they were surprised that a city politician of Layton's stature would put his credibility on the line to continue fighting what appeared to be a lost cause. Jack Layton told the Toronto activists they needed to work harder and to bring more people onside.

Hartmann says Layton's confidence stemmed from his fundamental belief that, if given all the facts, ordinary people would do the right thing. "He told us, we could still win this because the Adams Mine was a bad idea and because people in Ontario would speak up once they know what's at stake. His confidence was contagious."

The Algonquins Begin to Move

The pressure from Premier Harris at Toronto City Hall confirmed what many people in the north already knew—that the fix was in to push this project forward. As a show of pushing back, 2,800 people gathered for a rally at the Earlton Arena on July 28, 2000. The mood of this rally was much more militant than that of previous marches. Up until that moment, the strategy had been to draw in more people to the campaign by underplaying the notion of a potential confrontation. The Earlton rally was set up to send a message. The largest political rally the region had seen, it showcased the solid line of political leaders who were opposed to the dump. The rally spilled out from the arena and then formed into a march to the ONR rail lines in downtown Earlton, where the tracks were once

2,800 people march in the village of Earlton, as part of the Line in the Sand protest. July 28, 2000.

again blockaded. Farm tractors moved out onto Highway 11 to block any movement of vehicles.

A symbolic line in the sand was drawn across the tracks. "It's fair to say we will consider this [the Toronto vote] to be an aggressive declaration of war against Northern Ontario," declared Pierre Belanger. "We will take that as an aggressive move and we will take action. Toronto will be shamed."[11]

"This is a war," said MPP David Ramsay. "It is a fight for democracy." The language couldn't get any clearer. The question remained whether anyone outside of Timiskaming was actually listening.

The rally in Earlton showcased the growing strength of the anti-dump coalition. Nowhere was that strength more evident than in the appearance of two leaders from the Algonquin Nation (ten Bands that live along the lower and upper Ottawa River in Ontario and Quebec)—Anishinabeg Tribal Council Grand Chief Jimmy Hunter and Algonquin Nation Secretariat Grand Chief Carol McBride. McBride's home community of Timiskaming First Nation claimed territory that covered the region of central Timiskaming from New Liskeard up to the Adams Mine.

Throughout the Adams Mine regulatory process, the city and Notre kept the Aboriginal consultation focused on the Beaverhouse First Nation, a small landless Band whose members lived in the Kirkland Lake area. They had few resources for asserting their rights and were not even recognized under the Indian Act. Timiskaming First Nation, along with its larger political organization, the Algonquin Nation Secretariat, had long asserted Aboriginal title to the region in question. They established a strong paper trail documenting their efforts to be part of the consultation process as the province, city, and promoters pushed the proposal through the various regulatory channels.

Grand Chief McBride was a shrewd and determined leader. She followed carefully the advice of Band lawyer David Nahwegahbow, "Don't make a threat that you can't follow through on." Thus, the Algonquin Band Council at Timiskaming was determined that if they became involved in the fight they would bring all the political, legal, and on-the-ground resistance to bear that was necessary. McBride didn't seem like a radical leader. She had a huge personality and laughed easily. You might have mistaken her for a lovable auntie, but McBride was a skilled negotiator and, when it came time to step into the fight, she was ready to go all the way. Chief McBride quickly became the identified leader of the campaign. She threw herself into the battle, travelling up and down the highway to both Ottawa and Toronto with Pierre Belanger building allies.

The first move of the Algonquins was to push for a federal environmental assessment of the Adams Mine plan under Section 48 of the federal Environmental Assessment Act (impacts on lands and resources of a First Nation reserve). The threat wasn't just smoke. The case was solid and the federal government took the claim seriously. This move infuriated Gordon McGuinty. But the Algonquins weren't sweating the timelines of a promoter under the gun.

Alan McLaren, a spokesperson for the Algonquin Nation Secretariat, was matter-of-fact that the deal wasn't moving ahead without the support of the Algonquins. "Whatever contracts are signed, well it's too bad," he said. "We have legal interest in the land [and if the courts don't stop the project] . . . there's another step, we don't know what it will be, but it's going to be stopped one way or another."[12]

Did this mean blockades, the media asked. "For sure," he replied. "There's no two ways about it—the Adams Mine is not going ahead. We're going to stop it somewhere along the line, which will leave somebody holding the bag."

The language was bold and confrontational. It also had the potential to create discord among rural farm families and local prospectors who were just now learning that the Algonquin Nation was asserting title over lands they had long considered their own. The Timiskaming Algonquins had long been the "invisible people"[13] of the region. The non-Aboriginal community knew that TFN's assertion of land title at the Adams Mine could have long-term implications for future development in the region. But they also understood that there was no winning this fight without TFN's full participation.

In order to stop the dump, it was essential to establish a common front. We worked on the theory of the "big tent"—personal and political agendas had to be parked at the door. If you were against the dump, then you were welcome under the tent. Numerous meetings were held over the summer of 2000 to create understanding between the various communities—Aboriginal, Québécois, rural Ontarian.

At a meeting held in July 2000 at the Timiskaming First Nation community hall, John Vanthof admitted that, in the past, the non-Aboriginal community had paid little attention to the rights of the people living on reserve. "We came here asking your community to help us. We

Another Oka? Members of Timiskaming First Nation mount the Warrior flag on the Adams Mine rail crossing. PHOTO: courtesy of Sue Gamble

know that we haven't reached out before, but I promise that when this fight is over we will work with your community on the issues that remain unresolved." As summer turned into fall, the growing trust and friendship between the Aboriginal and non-Aboriginal coalition emerged as the real victory story of the campaign.

The involvement of the Algonquin Nation ratcheted up the stakes dramatically. The Wabun Tribal Council (representing Matachewan, Wahgoshig, and Mattagami First Nations) became more active. And then, Temagami First Nation declared its intention to stop the garbage trains from coming through its territory. At a rally on the shores of Lake Temagami, Regional Chief Charles Fox laid down the gauntlet.

> The Mike Harris government is driven by area codes 416 and 905. They don't give a shit about the north . . . they're throwing garbage on you for crying out loud. It's time we stood up to them . . . they want to ship the garbage by road and rail. Well, it's a long way from Toronto here and anything can happen.

Chief Raymond Katt reiterated Temagami First Nation's willingness to stop the trains. "This is a war between Northern and Southern Ontario." References to the recent First Nation confrontations at Burnt Church and Oka began to appear in the media. But this fight was different. This time blue-collar communities were standing side by side with First Nations. At a local rally, Martin Millen from Matachewan First Nation declared that the Native and non-Native would fight together.

> I think there are a lot of people in the north who are prepared to lay down their lives for it. People will physically get in there [Adams Mine] and they'll stop it. If no one listens, what else do you have to do? It's already happening at Burnt Church. Somebody has to do it and it won't be just natives. It will be all northerners.[14]

The Olympic Flame Gets Doused

The Toronto vote pushed Mayor Lastman into the spotlight as the key political driver of the Adams Mine project. It was Lastman's job to keep his council focused on the final vote slated to begin on October 1. But as the issue began to spiral faster and faster out of political containment, it was clear that Lastman wasn't up for the job.

The amiable, if somewhat hapless, mayor just didn't have the political smarts. Unlike Mike Harris and Gordon McGuinty, Mel Lastman wasn't built for confrontation. The furniture hawker turned politician didn't have the tactical skills needed to defuse a situation as complex and volatile as the Adams Mine. As he tried to circle the wagons at city hall, he began to make mistakes.

When pressed by the media about the threat of a confrontation with residents in the north, he shrugged it off, saying that northerners had begged for the garbage. "We didn't go to them," he said. "They came to us and said, 'we want your garbage.' In fact they were persistent. They didn't stop. They kept coming and they're still coming saying 'we want your garbage.'"[15] Councillor Giorgio Mammoliti picked up the theme and added fuel to the fire. "One man's trash is another man's treasure. They asked for our garbage. Who are we to say no?"[16]

Lastman's dismissive attitude was helping drive all manner of people in the north to get off the fence and join the fight against the dump. Pierre Belanger challenged Lastman directly in the media. "With the cavalier comments of Mel Lastman Toronto couldn't have declared its scorn for Northern Ontario more clearly if it had written it in plain scrawl on the front of city hall."[17]

But Lastman wasn't the only one with a political tin ear. *The Toronto Star* attempted to calm the waters by advising Lastman to be nicer to the side that was obviously set to lose. "It is time for some healing. Lastman would do this city and its reputation a favour if he were to go north and smooth the feathers he has ruffled."[18] Clearly the flagship paper of the largest city in the country didn't have a clue. This fight had moved well beyond ruffled feathers.

But Lastman wasn't concerned about northern resentment. He was focused on establishing Toronto as a "world-class" metropolis. Who cared what folks in Timiskaming or Timmins thought if you were noticed by L.A., London, and New York?

The road to world-class status lay in securing the 2008 Summer Olympics. In August 2000, Lastman sent a promotional team to the planning meeting of the International Olympic Committee (IOC) being held in Lausanne, Switzerland. He pitched the Toronto bid like it was a deal at his Bad Boy store. But much to the surprise of the Toronto bid team, the Adams Mine Coalition announced that they were also travelling to Switzerland. Pierre Belanger told sceptical national media that Toronto's Olympic bid was now a target.

> We're going to derail Toronto's bid to be the host of the 2008 Olympics. We're going to cause as many problems as we can for Toronto. We are going to make life miserable for Toronto bureaucrats and Toronto councillors. We are also marshalling the forces of Northern Ontario and the proud northerners. Northern Ontario will not be Southern Ontario's garbage dump.[19]

Terry Graves holding a press conference on the Adams Mine blockade.

Terry Graves was part of the northern delegation to Switzerland (all of whom paid their own fare). Graves had started his career in television in Hamilton. He came north because he loved the wilderness. He had been active in the 1989 logging blockade on the Red Squirrel Road in Temagami and was a founder of the Temiskaming Environmental Action Committee. His day job was paralegal to local litigation king Owen Smith, where Graves was a "fixer" like the George Clooney character in the film *Michael Clayton*. In a world of hard-asses, Graves was as hard as they come. He told the media in no uncertain terms that the attack on the Olympic bid was part of a strategy to make Toronto politicians rue the day they ever heard of Timiskaming.

"We spent 11 years trying to talk to Toronto Council and they wouldn't give us the time of day. We feel our efforts would be better spent explaining to the IOC why Toronto is unworthy of the games," Graves stated in an Adams Mine Coalition press release on August 23, 2000.

Under IOC rules, the potential host city must prove that it has a strong environmental record and is not facing local opposition to the games. Graves laid down the rules of engagement. "Over 300 million litres of our northern groundwater will be squandered every year washing garbage. Either the IOC has an environmental policy that they follow or they don't. We think the European community will look upon this project as incredibly wasteful."[20]

Grand Chief Carol McBride led the team to Lausanne. "We told Toronto we would do everything in our power to stop this dump," she said, explaining why a contingent from the Algonquin Nation had joined the Adams Mine Coalition in fighting Toronto's bid in Europe.

Mark Arsenault, of the Toronto Olympic bid team, was clearly worried but attempted to downplay the potential damage. He said he didn't want to venture into the dump debate, but "it's not something that's helpful to us."[21]

Helen Lenskyj, author of *Inside the Olympic Industry*, told *The Toronto Star* that the issue of the environment was a major vulnerability of the Toronto bid. "On the record, the IOC will say this is a small group of opponents [and] that it means nothing. But privately they'll say that it does. A group like that [Adams Mine Coalition] is able to say you have to be able to walk the walk where the environment is concerned."[22]

The media were initially amused at what they saw as a quixotic excursion on the part of the pesky Adams Mine fighters. But once in Europe, the protesters hooked up with members of European Greenpeace and declared their intention of dogging both the Toronto bid team and the IOC leadership. When Graves led the protest delegation right into the meeting of the IOC, the Toronto team knew it was in trouble.

In front of international media, Graves presented IOC president Juan Antonio Samaranch with thousands of letters denouncing the Toronto bid. The media were informed that the Adams Mine Coalition had already set up meetings with competing bid teams from Paris and other cities. At one point during this media confrontation, Dick Pound, Canada's point person at the ioc, took Graves aside and asked him, "Where are you taking this fight next?"

Graves responded, "When we're done here, we'll take the fight to the Vatican."

Pound shook his head, "This bid doesn't have a hope in hell."[23]

Toronto politicians now knew that the Adams Mine Coalition wasn't going to go away. The coalition was playing for keeps. Lastman's big dream of Olympic glory died that day and never recovered.

In the dog days of August 2000, activists in Toronto were working full out to wake people up to the looming environmental and PR disaster they were facing under Lastman. On the plus side, Torontonians were no friends of Mike Harris. But, on the other hand, time was running out and it was still difficult for some people to understand that a mine wasn't a safe place to store garbage. When urbanites heard the word Adams Mine, they conjured up images of a deep shaft with tunnels in impregnable rock. In a world before YouTube, Facebook, and Twitter, changing this perception wasn't easy.

A visual image of the pit would go a long way to changing the nature of the discussion. Clearly, the cost of billboards or media ads was out of the question. The war council decided to pay for a poster with a dramatic photograph of the natural beauty of the water-filled pit. The poster carried the simple slogan "Adams Mine: It Just Wouldn't Be the Same with Toronto's Garbage in It." Volunteer crews hit downtown Toronto with posters and glue buckets. The narrative in the city was moving steadily away from the question of whether the Adams Mine was a made-in-Ontario solution, to one of whether it was worth the risk to the groundwater in this artificial lake.

The other prop that helped draw public attention was a mascot—Mel the Moose, a wire-framed moose stuffed with garbage. Mel the Moose was the project of Alex Melaschenko's high school shop class at Timiskaming

District Secondary School in New Liskeard. Melaschenko had been drawn into action when he heard Lastman's comments about northern people asking for the garbage. He decided to have his students create a life-sized wire-framed moose to use as a mascot.

Mel the Moose was initially built to ridicule Lastman's tourism promotion scheme to fill Toronto with statues of multicoloured moose. The moose was the ultimate northern symbol, and yet Lastman was setting the north up as a garbage dump. Mel the Moose was seen locally as part joke, part "in your face" response to the Bad Boy Mayor. And yet, surprisingly enough, this mascot quickly became a hit with media and people outside the north. People loved to get their picture taken with Mel the Moose. Realizing we had stumbled on a great organizing tool, Mel was put on a flatbed truck and sent on numerous runs down Highway 11 and along Highway 17. Wherever Mel went, crowds gathered. Mel's back-up crew—Ambrose Raftis, Bob Wolfe, and Mel Booth—ensured that there were appropriate letters and petitions to sign. Many spin-off campaigns against the Adams Mine were started in communities thanks to Mel the Moose.

By the early fall of 2000, Mel the Moose was spending a great deal of time parked outside Parliament Hill. There were now two federal EA requests—one from the Algonquin Nation and one from the municipal associations of Abitibi-Témiscamingue, Quebec, who feared cross-border contamination along the shared waterway of Lake Timiskaming.

Pierre Brien, the Bloc Québécois MP for Abitibi region, was speaking out. The federal New Democratic Party caucus took up the fight, with MPs Alexa McDonough and Nelson Riis demanding action. This move pushed Timiskaming Liberal MP Benoît Serré to get onside. As Toronto residents became increasingly engaged, key urban Liberal MPs began lining up against Harris and Lastman. The fight was quickly spilling out beyond the carefully constructed sales pitch of Rail Cycle North.

5

The Rising of the Moon
September–October 2000

There are alliances that will never be broken. It will never be the
same again in this region. I have never been part of a community like
this. I love the fact that the project supporters didn't understand who
we are. They thought we weren't here. They thought it was just bush
and bears. They thought people here were nothing to reckon with.

—JOSEPH GOLD, October 2000

Preparing for Civil Disobedience

IT WAS FALL FAIR DAY in Englehart. The farmers were in the fields
working full out to get the harvest in before the cold October rains
cut through the yellowing birch leaves and canola fields. The fall fair
had deep roots in Englehart, and the newly formed Englehart Ratepayers
Association decided to use the day to hold a rally to oppose the dump.

Similar rallies were being held across the region and into neighbouring Quebec. Hundreds of people came out to a rally in picturesque Ville-
Marie, Quebec, on the shores of Lake Timiskaming. Quebec organizers
like Pierre Ayotte were building a powerful solidarity campaign in the

Abitibi-Témiscamingue region. Leaders from both sides of the border—no longer two solitudes—were meeting regularly.

These rallies would take on the character of the host town. Each town had its own particular culture and history. Englehart was a town founded by the railway, and many families were still actively involved in the freight and passenger operations of the Ontario Northland Railway.

But the folks who gathered in Railway Park were not willing to go along with the plan to ship garbage on the train. For this, they had been denounced as radicals and eco-terrorists, but it didn't intimidate the Englehart volunteers. One of these "radicals" was Maureen Connolly, a hard-working volunteer with the Ladies Auxiliary of the local Legion. Gladys Decker, another regular at the rallies, brought with her many friends from a local fundamentalist church.

As the Englehart rally got under way, a television news crew from Toronto was on the scene gathering footage for a documentary on the Adams Mine. They paid no attention to Rev. Mike Shute, who was warming up the crowd with the traditional call and response allegories of a rural Bible church. The message appeared to be lost on the news team, but it rang out clear as a bell to the people in the park.

"The time is coming when we will be asked to cross the river," he intoned. "When that time comes, will you be ready to cross over?" Those in the crowd from Evangelical backgrounds called out in the affirmative.

"When you have crossed that river, there will be no going back," he continued. "Are you ready to keep going?" "Amen," the people responded.

Like in any good sermon, he asked the salvation question, "When the time comes, will you be ready?" But Rev. Shute wasn't speaking of the Promised Land; he was asking the two hundred people in the park if they were willing to take the fight against the Adams Mine to the next level. This was a preparation drill for civil disobedience, and the response was as affirmative as the call to faith in any gospel hall on a rural back road.

When the time comes—the allusion to the coming showdown—was being used across Timiskaming. When provincial NDP leader Howard

Hampton spoke at a protest on the Adams Mine Road, Kirkland Lake resident Kathy Robinson confronted him directly. "It's all fine and well that you're here today," she said. "But will you be back on this road when the time comes?" Hampton said he would stand with northerners when push came to shove.

All summer long people came up to me at the local stores or Tim Hortons to assure me that "when the time comes" they could be counted on. Many of them were folks I had never met before. The decision to physically stop this project was not a step that anyone took lightly. There was nothing to gain personally and everything to lose by stepping forward to defy authorities. And yet, across the district, individuals and couples were taking the time to weigh the consequences and deciding that stopping the Adams Mine took precedence over their own personal security.

As I heard this whisper of resistance across the region, I thought of the old Irish rebel song:

> Out of many a mud-walled cabin eyes were watching through the night
> Many manly hearts were throbbing for the coming morning light
> Murmurs ran along the valley like the banshee's lonely croon
> And a thousand pikes were flashing by the rising of the moon

Barring a miracle, the rural north and the urban south were moving towards an inevitable confrontation. None of us had any real idea of what that confrontation would look like. A select subcommittee of the Adams Mine war council took the lead in mapping out some scenarios. All of them looked scary.

First off, we had to look at whom we were up against. It was one thing to take on Mel Lastman and Toronto City Council, but if the vote for the dump passed, locals would be facing off against the provincial police under the direction of Premier Harris. Harris thrived on confrontation. One of his first acts as premier had been to make an example out of Aboriginal protesters from Stony Point First Nation who had occupied Ipperwash

Provincial Park over a long-standing land dispute. "I want the fucking Indians out of the Park," he is reported to have declared.[1] Soon after, protester Dudley George was killed by an OPP officer. No one expected that Harris would be any more accommodating with protesters threatening his pet project.

The second issue was where such a showdown should take place. Setting up a blockade on the isolated mine road—seven kilometres of winding gravel—presented numerous logistical problems. But you don't always get to choose your battlefield. In the leaky pits of the Adams Mine was where the garbage was going to end up, and so, scary or not, Chief Carol McBride was adamant that the road to the pits was where the local opposition would make its stand.

I had spent all summer thinking about the coming blockade on the Adams Mine Road. I knew that music could play a big role in keeping people focused. The problem, however, is that many of the songs in the canon of protest had become clichéd or out of date. On that Saturday in Englehart, I unveiled what I hoped would become our region's rallying song:

> We gave you all our silver, we gave you all our gold
> And you crippled all our rivers for the hydro that they hold,
> We gave you all our White Pine and our young ones as they grew
> But we'll never give the watershed, no matter what you do.

As I looked into the crowd, I saw that some people were crying as they sang along. But it wasn't because they were sad. These were people who were ready to go the distance. I had written the music, but they had been living the reality for years. "The Adams Mine Song" was quickly adopted as our anthem. In the coming months, it would be sung at rallies, blockades, and Toronto City Hall council chambers.[2]

On September 20, the Adams Mine Coalition ran the following full-page advertisement in *The Temiskaming Speaker*:

Charlie Angus singing "The Adams Mine Song"—the anthem of the blockade. PHOTO: courtesy of Barb Biederman-Bukowski

Mel Lastman told the people of Toronto that you begged for their garbage. Gordon McGuinty says you'll be a willing host for Toronto garbage.

IT'S TIME TO SHOW THE WORLD THAT WE WILL NEVER BE TORONTO'S GARBAGE PICKERS. MARK DOWN OCTOBER 1ST IN YOUR CALENDAR. A DAY TO MAKE HISTORY.

Stay tuned for important details and further instructions. We have said time and time again that the garbage will never come!

THE TIME HAS COME!

You are the only thing left standing between Toronto's garbage and the water of Temiskaming.

No other details were provided. None were needed. 'Twas the rising of the moon.

Shutting Down the Road

The showdown began very matter-of-factly, almost like a community barn raising. Early on the morning of Sunday, October 1, volunteer crews led by Barry Story showed up with chainsaws and weed whackers, and started clearing a section of bush about three kilometres up the Adams Mine Road. There was no natural spot on this twisting road to set up any kind of sizable camp. The terrain was little more than swamp and rock cuts on an ever-ascending, winding road to the hill that hosts the Adams Mine. Nonetheless, this was going to be where we made our stand and the community was determined to make the best of it.

As the saws cut away the dogwood and poplars, flatbeds pulled up with loads of straw bales. A load of donated lumber came next. The supplies were used to create a makeshift set of benches for the crowds expected to begin coming up the road by noon.

By one o'clock, a crowd of seven hundred gathered in the newly created field by the road. The summer of marching had led to this point. Like all Adams Mine rallies, the symbols of unity and regional solidarity were in full array. The Timiskaming First Nation's Saugeen Drummers welcomed people to the land the Algonquins had renamed Mamowedewin (Coming Together). Speeches in French and English underlined the unity of Ontarians and their Quebec neighbours. "There is no ugly Toronto councillor who is going to decide our fate. We're making a stand—Quebecers, First Nations, and Ontarians," declared Pierre Belanger.

And then the speeches gave way to an ecumenical prayer service. Joseph Gold led a prayer with his rabbinical prayer shawl. He was followed by Rev. Mike Shute and Elder Jim Twain from Temagami First Nation. As Twain prepared a traditional Aboriginal smoke smudge, Shute called on God to provide support for those stepping forward to engage in civil disobedience. A large group solemnly stood in line for what was to be, for most of them, the first traditional Aboriginal ceremony they had ever participated in.

With this solemn moment over, Grand Chief Carol McBride gave the orders to the crowd. "We've got a big fight on our hands. We need everybody. We are making history. Let's prepare for the fight. We're going to win it."

And with that, they moved an RV across the road leading to the mine and began erecting a barricade of timber. Most of the crowd went home to Sunday supper until further instructions were given. A smaller vanguard—a mixed bunch including nurse Fran Nychuk, logger Vince Auger, and retired teachers Dennis and Kathy Hakola—were left behind to set up tents for the occupation of the road.

A large team from Timiskaming First Nation was on hand. It was clear that, from this point on, TFN would play a huge role in whatever happened on the road. Grand Chief McBride was backed up by Councillor Gerald "Sonny Boy" Hanberry and a crew of foot soldiers including Kevin Stanger, Willie Groulx, Darryl McBride, Simon Chief, and Sean McLaren. TFN Band manager Mark Hall was onsite to support Chief McBride and her councillors. Hall, a former Royal Ulster Constabulary officer from Belfast, Ireland, was happy to be as far from the Belfast troubles as he could get, but his accent was stamped with the intonation of confrontation. During one meeting between McBride and the OPP, Hall astounded local law officials when he spoke up with a brogue that sounded like it had stepped right off the Shankill Road on the twelfth of July. "I'm telling ye," he said, "noothin' is gooin' up tha' road until we say it diz."

Nonetheless, the first night on the road passed without confrontation. Terry Graves emerged as the lead negotiator for the blockades. The police established a pattern of engaging in two separate lines of negotiations. The OPP negotiated with Graves regarding the locals on the blockade, while the RCMP and OPP negotiated with Chief McBride regarding the First Nation presence. The police and the blockade leadership knew the importance of maintaining frank but open lines of communication. As tensions on the road increased, this situation could get out of hand very quickly.

The morning after the blockade went up on the Adams Mine Road, the farmers launched a second front twenty-five kilometres south of the mine. As police were focused on the mine road, the farm community set up a daylong blockade of the ONR line near Frank Rivard's dairy farm at Earlton.

Rivard had never done a radical thing in his life. But when interviewed by CBC national television, he declared emphatically that garbage trains would never make it past his farm. "If they start shipping the garbage, we'll be here. A train is the easiest thing to stop. Would you quit? This is my life here. I can't quit."

The farmers blocked the tracks with farm vehicles. They then built a massive "train" of hay bales in one of the fields. An effigy of Mel Lastman as the conductor was placed on top of the hay. "Mel doesn't give a damn about us," Rivard explained, "so we are showing we don't give a damn about him and his garbage problem."

Tiger torches were lit up and the bales quickly caught fire. The ominous smoke filtered across the rolling fields of Earlton.

Police moved in from surrounding detachments to monitor this second blockade. As police and farmers stood facing each other on the rail line, it began to rain. A tent was set up and some folks brought out barbeques. As the burger patties hit the grills, the police were invited to get shelter from the rain. After all, farmers like Louis Ethier, Robin Flewelling, Carman Kidd (future mayor of Temiskaming Shores), and Chris Brazeau were their neighbours. Their kids played hockey together. In fact, some local police officers spent their off-hours volunteering against the dump. It was all very friendly, but both sides knew it was a very serious business.

At four in the afternoon, John Vanthof announced that the time had come to remove the blockade. Some farmers began to grumble. "We've got the line shut, it should stay shut," they declared. Vanthof was emphatic. "We told the police that this would be an afternoon shutdown. We will keep our word."

Ending the blockade at four didn't convey a sense of weakness or half-heartedness. It was meant to show the discipline of the region. Both sides understood the underlying message—the people living along the tracks would decide the movement of the trains. Today the trains were being allowed to continue; tomorrow could be a different story.

In Toronto, the council was convening what would be a fractious session. *Globe and Mail* columnist John Barber predicted that Lastman was walking into a disaster: "The Adams Mine is no longer merely a risky, expensive and unnecessary mega-project. Judging by the nationwide opposition it is shaping up as an environmental disgrace. A giant black eye for Toronto. We can see the punch coming and we're walking right into it. "[3]

The pressure on Lastman was enormous. As a numbers game, the fight was a done deal. Lastman had the support of a majority of City Council. However, the opposition councillors (led by Jack Layton, Olivia Chow, David Miller, Michael Walker, Jane Pitfield, and Sandra Bussin) were better organized. They also had time on their side. For every day they dragged out the debate, the pressure became that much more intense. Municipal elections were barely a month away, and as city residents grew increasingly restless about the Adams Mine plan, pro-dump councillors found themselves voting against their own political future.

In an attempt to derail the opposition, Lastman embargoed key details of the deal from the council. The move backfired on the pro–Adams Mine councillors. "That's just shocking," said Layton. "This is a $1 billion deal and right now we have blindfolds on. What they're asking us to do is to sign and approve the largest secret contract in the history of municipal government in Canada and that's not right."[4]

The debate began on October 1 and City Council chambers were packed with Toronto residents deeply opposed to the project. Long-time city activists had been successful in portraying Adams Mine as a backward solution. As long as the city could find huge holes to dump waste, it would never get serious about the need for recycling and waste diversion.

Environmental activist Tooker Gomberg emerged during this period as a champion of waste diversion. He denounced Lastman for being a laggard on waste issues and pointed to the example of Edmonton with its ambitious recycling and waste diversion plans.

As the pro–Adams Mine councillors attempted to sell the deal, Larry Jensen, the former provincial geologist for the Adams Mine region, came out of retirement to fight the project. Dr. Jensen had the credibility that Notre's consultants lacked. He had seen the bottom of the pits. He had studied the flows of water at the mine. And now, on the eve of the Toronto Council vote, he was challenging Mayor Lastman in a very public way.

In a letter written to Toronto Council, Jensen declared: "The Adams Mine Garbage Dump Proposal is a disaster. . . . [It has the] high potential to pollute an area many times the size of Toronto, [this] may be economically expedient but it is morally unconscionable."[5]

He reached out to every councillor in Toronto, Durham, Peel, and York, challenging them over the dangers posed by the project. Jensen's appearance came as word was in the air that the federal government was about to intervene with an environmental assessment. Key Toronto Liberal MPs were now speaking out against the deal. Lastman wasn't taking the pressure well. *The Toronto Star*, which had been bullish on the deal in the summer, was now calling on the mayor to pull back from the brink.

> Holding the vote now would be a serious mistake. Councillors aren't ready to make an informed choice. They haven't been briefed on the final contract negotiated by City staff. By late yesterday, none of them had even received copies of the deal. . . . This is the biggest contract most councillors will ever vote on. It's critical that they take the time to do it right.[6]

Blake Kinahan was the first councillor to jump from the slate of dump supporters. Frances Nunziata cut herself loose as well. The media was reporting off-the-record comments from Lastman's team, who blamed the mayor for botching the selling of the deal.[7]

When Councillor Raymond Cho made it known that he was thinking of ditching the Adams Mine slate, Lastman ran across the council chamber and shouted into the startled councillor's face, "Are you breaking with me on this?"[8]

The relentless questions and procedural wrangling were wearing on the nerves of the Lastman crew. Pro-dump councillor Milton Berger barked at anti-dump councillor Pam McConnell that she should "go home and bake cookies."[9] This comment resulted in an uproar from the packed gallery. Jack Layton led the crowd in clapping and chanting against Berger. In the battle for hearts and minds, the bumbling Bad Boy Mayor was proving a less-than-impressive general.

Stopping the Train

From the vantage point of the Adams Mine Road, it was hard to tell if Toronto was feeling the northern pressure at all. Some national media covered the blockade, but most of their attention was focused on the debate at Toronto City Hall. The driving principle behind our 2000 campaign had been to set the agenda. But now, we found ourselves ensconced on an abandoned mine road while six hundred kilometres away, Mayor Lastman was deciding the fate of the region.

In the early morning of October 3, a group of about forty protesters gathered to decide how to ratchet up the pressure yet again. The only available choice was to blockade the rail line itself. All traffic for the Ontario Northland Railway crossed the Adams Mine Road at a juncture roughly one kilometre down from the blockade camp.

There would be nothing symbolic about shutting down the rail line. This was serious business. Everyone knew it. If the trains were stopped for more than a few hours, the economic costs for the ONR and numerous northern enterprises would be felt immediately. The largest stress would be on the massive regional copper smelters in Timmins and across the

Adams Mine blockade on the Ontario Northland rail tracks. October 2000.

provincial border in Rouyn-Noranda. They relied on the ONR to move hundreds of tanker cars filled with sulphuric acid. How long the smelters could continue running without the movement of the acid trains was anyone's guess.

As people gathered in the field, Brenda Gold led the discussion. The meeting held a cross-section of ages and backgrounds. Seventy-five-year-old Lloyd Wilson, a stalwart of the New Liskeard Presbyterian Church, stood beside Oka veteran Kevin Stanger. The discussion was short and to the point. If the trains were stopped, arrests were almost guaranteed. And then, if the leadership was arrested, how would the resistance continue? No one had an answer. We were facing the abyss, but this was the moment people had been psychologically preparing for for months—in some cases, for years.

The coalition had tried to build a disciplined army of northerners. And so, protesters fell in line behind a parade of four flag-bearers carrying the flags of Canada, Ontario, Quebec, and Timiskaming First Nation. The makeshift parade marched down the road to the rail crossing. Stopping a train isn't an easy thing to do, and no one knew what to expect. Just before the group stepped on the tracks, an Englehart farmer asked everyone to pause. He had never spoken up before at a rally, and there was a slight tremor of emotion in his voice.

"I just want to say," he stammered, "like, whatever happens next, there's a story I thought people should hear." And then, like a kid at Bible class, he began to relate the story of Moses and Joshua in the fight against King Amalek. As long as Moses held his arm in the air, the battle went their way. When Moses became tired and the arm started to slip, the battle turned against them. "So the people held up Moses' arm," he said. "And that's how they won the battle." Then he paused. "That's all I wanted to say."

And with that the protesters stepped onto the railbed and walked north along the tracks. Almost immediately we ran into an ONR maintenance vehicle. Barry Story stepped forward and informed them that the Ontario Northland rail line was now closed. A few straw bales were symbolically placed at the intersection of the road and rail. An initial team of volunteers including Joseph Gold, Bob Wolfe, Leigh Muething, and Fran Patterson sat on the tracks and waited for arrest. As word spread that the trains had been stopped, more people began arriving from across the district.

As the day wore on, tents began to pop up. Members from Timiskaming First Nation set up tents and a large communal fire. Kirkland Lakers Shirley Dorsey, Anne Dmytruk, Jacqueline Fortier, and Joyce McEwen began hauling in cooking supplies. Volunteers showed up with a wonderful array of homemade cabbage rolls, lasagna, and beans.

In the late afternoon, a truck pulled up to the barricade and a team of volunteers from Ville-Marie, Quebec, jumped out. They brought with them fifty pounds of fresh fish from Lake Timiskaming that they had loaded up as soon as they heard the news that the train line was shut down.

An eagle circled over the tracks—a very good omen for the Algonquin protesters.

There were now over a hundred people on the railbed. The OPP were monitoring the situation from a makeshift post three hundred feet down from the tracks. No one knew what was going to happen next. When local media pressed OPP sergeant Don Goard as to whether the police had a plan, he replied honestly, "Well, there are a lot of plans. Plan A, Plan B, Plan C. But nothing is solid for sure. We'll just wait and see what happens. We'd like to resolve this without having to do any arrests. Our number one concern is the safety of our officers and the safety of those people."

By the next morning, the rail line was beginning to look like a town of tents. Police negotiated with Terry Graves and Chief McBride separately through the day. People from across the region were pouring in to take shifts on the blockade. Everyone knew that arrests could come at any time. Seventy-seven-year-old Ina Phippen was joined by her sixty-three-year-old friend Loni Lucas. "I'm not afraid to be arrested," said Phippen. "I believe with all of my heart that what I am doing is right."[10]

Joseph Gold told the crowd they were part of a much larger fight. "We are up against some very powerful financial and political forces," he said. "It is an uphill battle but a lot of small people are surprisingly strong. If we can stop the trains as we did, why can't we stop the trains when garbage is in them?"[11]

Protester Earl Collingridge knew the people of the region. He had been playing fiddle at square dances at the various country halls across Timiskaming for more than sixty years. Collingridge told the media that the Adams Mine Road was now permanently shut to garbage. "If they can't get the message, they're pretty dumb. We've never been a willing host."[12]

More and more First Nation members began to arrive from regional reserves. The cookhouse grew. Many people slept in their cars. Bonnie Borden moved into the tent town. This retired real estate agent turned artist may have seemed like an unlikely radical. But she was a local gal who wasn't averse to roughing it on the road.

As the number of protesters grew, police were seconded from detachments across the north. Many patrolled the rail lines for possible sabotage. The overall atmosphere on the blockade appeared to be very friendly, but everyone knew the situation was volatile.

At the local Tim Hortons in Kirkland Lake, police reinforcements and day shift blockade volunteers often stood side by side waiting for their Timbits and double-doubles. On the third morning of the rail blockade, a police officer leaned over to one protester and whispered, "Tell your people to clear the track. Make sure everything is moved off the rail line."

When the information was passed on to the organizers, Terry Graves gave the order to immediately comply. It was apparent the police had been given orders to move against us because of impediments on the rail line. The straw bales were moved. The lawn chairs were put to the side. One volunteer even took out a broom and swept off the loose bits of straw.

When Graves went up the road for his morning meeting with the OPP, they confronted him with a demand to immediately clear the tracks or face arrest. He shrugged. "We're not blocking the tracks. Look for yourself."

The lead officer peered through his binoculars to see clean tracks and a waving crowd of protesters standing beside them. The tracks had been cleared, though the ONR still couldn't move the trains with so many protesters camped out beside the rail line. The blockade had bought one more day.

The protesters and the police were engaged in a very delicate power dance. The OPP were more than willing to do their job, but some chafed at being used as Harris's shock troops against their northern neighbours. They had been used by Premier Harris to clear the Aboriginal protest at Ipperwash, but when First Nation activist Dudley George was killed, it was an OPP officer who took the fall. As well, the OPP had taken considerable criticism for their role in a March 18, 1996, confrontation with anti-Harris protesters at Queen's Park.

The OPP knew that the Adams Mine standoff had turned Timiskaming into a tinderbox. If police did initiate mass arrests against the leadership, how would they prevent this protest from going rogue and going to ground? Even Liberal MPP David Ramsay was warning about an escalating conflict. "[The garbage] will never arrive. I can promise you that. There are 39 bridges and 600 kms of tracks—that is just not something you can control."[13] As long as the energy was focused on the road, such rogue acts might be contained.

Looking back on the blockade, Joe Muething says the police had a major problem because of the social complexity of the protest. "On the one hand, there was a whole lot of young guys from the reserve and the police had no idea how far these young guys would go. On the other hand, they had all these old ladies waddling in with hot muffins and breakfast to feed these young guys. It was a no-win situation for the cops."

Senior police officers from both the OPP and RCMP were in constant touch with Grand Chief McBride. They knew well that the Adams Mine was on the verge of becoming a lightning rod for frustrated young Warriors across Canada. In fact, we later learned that one Aboriginal "volunteer" who arrived from outside the area was an RCMP agent. Not that we would have changed our tactics if we'd known.

During one meeting, the RCMP asked McBride, "How long can you remain in control of this situation?"

"We can keep the discipline intact until the deal is signed," she said honestly. "But if Toronto signs that contract, I don't have any way of controlling who comes here or what happens next."

In some ways, allowing the protesters to stay on the road and rail line provided a pressure valve that police could monitor. Premier Harris didn't see it in the same light. On late Thursday, October 5, the eve of the Thanksgiving weekend, I was contacted by a source close to the regional

Crown attorney's office. "The premier is freaking out," the source said. "He is demanding at least a hundred arrests. He wants people to be held over the upcoming Thanksgiving weekend and kept in jail until next Tuesday."

Lastman was desperate to bring the vote to a conclusion. The anti–Adams Mine council members had already dragged the debate into the second week. Civic elections were coming within the month. If protesters were still holding the road after the Thanksgiving weekend, it would cause major problems. I asked, "Has the Crown attorney signed the warrants?" I knew Crown attorney Ron Davidson. He was a straight shooter with a deep streak of integrity.

The source replied, "Ron met with Judge [J. Douglas] Bernstein and they agreed they would take no moves against local people on the blockade unless things get out of hand."

We had bought ourselves another day. This had been the strategy throughout the blockade—to maintain the pressure day by day. But it was clear the police were being pushed to action.

On the Friday evening, a large crowd was gathered in the tent town. There was music and storytelling around the bonfires. Steve Patterson (future member of the Souljazz Orchestra) entertained us with blues sax with his father Dave playing guitar. Local residents Daisy Fannin and Rita McBride sang traditional country songs. It felt like a festival, and people had joined the protest from as far away as Toronto and Thunder Bay. A couple from Florida ventured down the road and decided to spend the evening.

The evening seemed remarkably lighthearted until *Toronto Sun* reporter Alan Cairnes took me aside and gave me the heads-up that the police were moving against the blockade. He had purchased a pizza for the desk girl at the hotel where the OPP were bunking. She gave him the intel that the wake-up call for Saturday morning had been set for 4:30 a.m.

"The cops are coming before dawn tomorrow to arrest you people. My paper hates you guys, but you're fighting the good fight. You have no idea how much damage you have done to the other side. No matter what happens, you have to be still standing here when the voting resumes on Tuesday."

To hold the line until next Tuesday. It seemed like an impossible task.

Night fell dark on the surrounding bush, but an eerie light appeared just beyond the curve in the road behind the police lines, emanating from the police cars and vans lining up for a raid on Thanksgiving Saturday morning. I wondered how it would be possible to hold the line until Tuesday.

I was standing with my wife watching the police congregate to begin marching at first light. Brit was holding our youngest daughter, Lola, who was two. Carol McBride came up to us and said simply, "It's either a really good sign or a really bad sign to see a mother with a baby on a blockade." Either way, we were about to find out.

Roasting the Pig

Just before dawn on October 7, the police set up their own blockade at the entrance to the Adams Mine Road. Any cars attempting to turn up the road from Highway 112 were turned back. But none of them left. They parked along the gravel shoulder of the highway, waiting determinedly until the police let them through. The biggest issue facing the police on that line was whether or not to allow the sixty-pound pig past the array of paddy wagons and police cars.

One frazzled officer received a lecture from an older couple from Kirkland Lake. "George Mangotich is roasting the Thanksgiving pig," they told him. "If you don't make room for his supplies, he's not going to be able to have the pig ready in time for the supper."

Behind the roast pig were families bringing turkey, ham, and lots and lots of pumpkin pie. Alerted that the OPP was moving in, organizers had relied on a decentralized rural phone tree to spread the word:

rather than bring placards or balaclavas, bring food and supplies for a massive Thanksgiving supper. Arrests or no arrests, we were going to celebrate Thanksgiving on the Adams Mine Road. Calls had also gone out the previous night to journalists to ensure that if there were going to be arrests, they would take place under the cameras of the national media.

At first light, the police came down in a phalanx to the railway tracks. We were already lined up on the other side, locked arm and arm. A police officer stepped out and read the injunction ordering us to leave. Terry Graves went forward to meet the officer, who tried to serve him with the injunction.

Graves looked it over and noticed that the official red seal was missing. "Wait a minute, this isn't a legitimate injunction. It came off a bloody fax machine. Where's the original?"

The original copy was nowhere to be had because the police couldn't find a local judge to sign it. They had been forced to rely on an injunction faxed from another jurisdiction. "You can't arrest us with a faxed injunction," Graves declared.

The officer repeated his ultimatum. Graves turned his back on the police. "I refuse to be a participant in an illegal act."

The police officer was now thoroughly confused. Tensions were running very high. Archie Wabie from Timiskaming First Nation began waving the Mohawk Warrior flag.

The police might be waiting for the better part of the day for an enforceable injunction to arrive. At this moment, officer Jim McDonnell, the lead commander for the OPP, stepped forward. He was all brass and serious business, and had been sent from North Bay Detachment to bring the situation under control.

McDonnell was a tough cop. I knew him because he was a huge fan of Canadian roots music, in particular the music of Fred Eaglesmith. Terry Graves was also a follower of Eaglesmith. During one of the short breaks in negotiations, I told Terry that McDonnell was a fellow "Fred head." Despite the extreme tension we were under, Graves broke into a smile. As he went forward for another round of negotiations, he stared in McDonnell's face and whispered, "I like trains. I like fast trains that call out through the rain."

McDonnell blinked; these were the words to a well-known Eaglesmith song. "Wait a minute," he protested. "You can't start quoting Fred in the middle of this."

A shared love of great Canadian music helped to break the tension. Both men were trying to find a way out of a potentially explosive situation. Graves knew the police had to open up the train line. Our objective was to find a way to stay on the road into the coming week.

McDonnell had a problem on his hands. He could easily fill the paddy wagons with Thanksgiving families, but that could lead to a troublesome backlash. Throughout the region, there could be many rural or First Nation loners willing to take matters into their own hands. Both sides feared a local "Wiebo Ludwig" guerilla campaign. And these fears were well grounded— within two days of the trains resuming, MPP David Ramsay would have to issue a public plea not to interfere with the trains or place debris along the 350 kilometres of tracks. (Fortunately, individual acts of disobedience remained largely symbolic, and no one was injured.)

McDonnell and Graves struck a compromise: the tent city was to be moved back fifty feet and days of backed-up freight allowed to move. The tents, cookhouses, and so on could stay on the road, leaving a de facto occupation of the Adams Mine Road intact. ONR officials were less than happy with the compromise, but McDonnell barked out the orders to push everything back fifty feet. Our volunteer army sprang into action. We couldn't believe we were still standing.

As Graves and McDonnell finalized their negotiations, people began pouring down the road with supplies for the single largest Thanksgiving supper Timiskaming had ever seen. Large temporary dining halls were built with two-by-fours and tarps to provide some protection from the increasingly cold temperatures.

The event began with prayers of Thanksgiving from the back of a pickup truck. Yellow birch leaves fell from the trees and swirled in the cold air as Rita McBride sang a haunting a cappella version of "Amazing Grace." And then the feeding of the thousand began. In true rural style, the gathered community came together in shared food and fellowship. The Thanksgiving meal on the Adams Mine Road was the highlight in a month of tension and conflict.

But as families celebrated their continued control of the road, the Adams Mine leadership realized we had come to another dead end. The Toronto vote was within three days, and we appeared to have run out of tools for maintaining the pressure.

As the Thanksgiving crowd gathered at the cookhouse, regional leaders of the movement met in an RV trailer to try and figure what to do next. The meeting of leaders included David Ramsay, Pierre Belanger, Barry Story, Chief Carol McBride, Kirkland Lake mayor Richard Denton, Joseph and Brenda Gold, and Terry and Eva Graves. All of the ideas that were floated seemed desperate, far-fetched, or insufficient. The success of our movement had depended on finding creative alternatives when our path was blocked. This time the obstacles appeared enormous. With an injunction against actions on the rail line, we would simply be sacrificing protesters to arrest and hardship if we stayed focused on the train. McBride listened quietly to each idea put forward. She then said emphatically, "Load up the school buses, we are taking the fight to Toronto."

There was a flurry of protests as to why this wasn't a good idea. But she was resolute. It was pretty clear that the Grand Chief of the Algonquin people had taken on the role of grand chief of this campaign.

The very next day, a short public meeting was held in the upstairs of Earlton Arena. Leftover food from the Thanksgiving dinner, including hundreds of slices of pumpkin pie, was laid out on the tables. The room quickly filled with hundreds of people, and the OPP stood along the walls of the hall. They seemed relieved that they didn't have to arrest us. The mood of the hall was energized.

Carol McBride stood up and made a simple pitch. "There are school buses outside," she declared. "We are leaving in one hour. We want you on those buses. Go home; get your toothbrush and your sleeping bag. We're going to take this fight right into the city of Toronto."

Three school buses quickly filled up with volunteers. Another group stayed behind to ensure the blockade on the road remained in place. Those who got on the buses had no idea where they were going to stay. No one seemed worried. As the buses made their way to Toronto, I made calls to every media outlet that I knew in the country. This was the moment of showdown and everyone knew it.

Just as we were entering Toronto city limits, we received a call from Jack Layton inviting us to stay at his campaign office in Riverdale. When the buses arrived, Layton, fellow councillor Olivia Chow, and MPP Marilyn Churley had laid out wine and food to welcome us. It was a great moment of hospitality. The floors weren't very comfortable to sleep on, but after a week of sleeping on a bush road facing the risk of arrest, nobody seemed bothered. Timiskaming was on the move.

The Toronto Showdown

IT'S NOT GOING NORTH. IT'S NOT GOING NORTH. The chants rang out through the City Council chambers all day Tuesday, October 10. Toronto City Council was under siege and the nation was watching. Over a hundred protesters from Northern Ontario had been met and welcomed by hundreds of Torontonians. Some were long-time veterans of city hall fights, but many others, like Toronto mother Louise Dunford,[14] came down to show their personal opposition to the plan. Deputy Mayor Case Ootes lamely attempted to keep order, but the chanting, singing, and fighting with security guards in the stands continually derailed attempts to move the Adams Mine vote forward.

Throughout the chaos of the morning session, Grand Chief Carol McBride sat in the first row of the public gallery showing no emotion or expression. She was surrounded by a large coterie of political supporters—MPPs Howard Hampton, Gilles Bisson, Marilyn Churley, and David Ramsay, Bloc MP Pierre Brien, and Liberal MP Benoît Serré. But all eyes were on her.

In early September, McBride had publicly asked for a meeting with the mayor. Lastman ducked the request. Just a few nights before, a CBC national news show had interviewed McBride and Pierre Belanger on the blockade about Lastman. "For three days before we came here [to the blockade] I tried calling Mayor Lastman, trying to talk to him as leader to leader," McBride quietly stated. "But he keeps putting me off. I guess he has no respect for the First Nations."

"But," added Belanger, "I think we're about to find that Mayor Lastman is in for a crash course in Canadian human relations."

And now the moment had arrived. As the council meeting chaotically rambled on, reporter John Northcott took Terry Graves aside and let him know that CBC was going to cut to national live coverage of the council proceedings at 11 a.m. If McBride was going to confront Lastman, this was the moment. Graves gave the heads-up to McBride while I organized a group of young Algonquin men—all in leather jackets and red baseball caps. My instructions were simple, "When Terry gives the signal, you are to walk down to the front of the council chambers, lock arms, and ensure that nobody gets to the Chief until she finishes speaking."

At eleven o'clock, Graves stood up in the council chambers and raised his arm. One by one, the young First Nation men made their way to the front and formed a phalanx. Security and police didn't move. Everyone in the council chamber stopped talking.

Carol McBride then stood up and, like a mother calling out a school-boy, laid into Lastman with shocking fury and determination. Lastman looked frightened and small. She warned him that the garbage would never come north. She told him that his declaration of war against the north would be met with hundreds, if not thousands, of people.

McBride then turned her attention to Gordon McGuinty, who had been lying low in the upper level of the city hall chamber. She challenged him and bedlam ensued. People were shouting. The cops appeared frozen. It seemed for a moment as if the entire City Council was going to fall over the precipice into chaos and fighting. And then McBride turned to the hundreds of people behind her in the stands. "Sit down," she shouted. "We are staying."

And with that, the crowd dutifully complied. Deputy Mayor Ootes continued on with the meeting, but it was clear who was in charge. The media captured the look on Lastman's face as he cringed at McBride's lecture. In that moment, his political career—though he would squeeze out one last re-election against environmental candidate Tooker Gomberg—was effectively over.

The media swarmed McBride. "What kind of message are you trying to send?"

McBride was fiery. "We are a force to be reckoned with, and this is only a little bit of our people. This deal will never happen."[15]

A *Toronto Sun* profile captured the paradox of Carol McBride, who appeared to be both a nurturing Earth mother and a radical leader.

> She used the O word. "This will make Oka look like a picnic," she said. "The city has declared war," she said.
>
> If the comments sound edgy and hysterical, the woman certainly isn't. There's such a mournful stillness about her, she startles you. While others fidget and squirm, she folds her hands, looks at you calmly with shrewd brown eyes and explains that she'll "do whatever I have to do. The garbage has to pass right in front of our homes. We have ways and means that it won't get where it's going."

She's a large woman, dressed in dark slacks and she looks immutable—a rock parting a river. And although her words could be interpreted as a threat, they sound simply matter of fact.[16]

McBride and Belanger remained in the city hall chambers throughout the 8½-hour debate. She wore a loose-fitting black dress adorned with a splash of pale flowers. He was dressed in a business suit with striped black and red tie. The matriarch and patriarch of the north looked like they were dressed for an afternoon church tea. Their aura of small-town reasonableness provided Canadians with a compelling counterpoint to a situation that appeared to be spiralling towards the brink.

Throughout the afternoon, the tensions grew in the chamber, and that evening, the national news flashed images of young First Nation men fighting in the council stands with security guards. Any doubts that urban Canada and the rural north were on the verge of confrontation were quickly dispelled as the fists flew in the hall of Crombie, Eggleton, and Sewell.

The city councillors knew they were losing control. Down on the council floor, opponents relied on filibuster and debate to push back against the wounded Lastman juggernaut. At one point, Councillor Sandra Bussin, who was in the anti–Adams Mine camp, stood up and read a thirty-one-page motion containing 623 clauses. When Ootes attempted to have her stop reading and simply submit the document, councillors tied up another hour of debate on the democratic rights of members.

Olivia Chow used her time to show a Simpsons episode that was eerily similar to the Adams Mine saga, with Homer Simpson playing the Gordon McGuinty role and Springfield becoming home to a toxic dump site in an abandoned mine on Native land. The Simpsons provided the one light note in an otherwise fractious and bitter day.

It was just a few weeks to the municipal election, and many councillors realized that by supporting the dump they were flushing their own political futures down the drain. Torontonians were becoming increasingly angry about the project, and the smarter councillors were jumping off the garbage train or running for cover. Environmental activist Gord Perks put the political hex on Works chair Bill Saundercook by vowing to have him defeated in the coming municipal election.

Lastman was in the vice. His councillors were taking a pounding from constituents and from the red-hot media glare. He could easily count on the right-wingers like Norm Gardner, George Mammoliti, and Doug Holyday. But other Lastman fair-weather councillors like Mario Silva and Brad Duguid stayed onside because Rail Cycle North (having secured a peek at the Republic bid) was offering to ship waste for eighty-one cents a tonne cheaper than Republic's conventional landfill opportunity in Michigan.

Behind the scenes, the Harris government was applying enormous pressure to stay the course. As *Globe and Mail* columnist John Barber pointed out, Lastman was sinking his political capital into the Adams Mine Pit.

> Not only is every conceivable red light flashing, the alternatives are easily available. The risks of going ahead are enormous. So what is the real reason Mel is determined to see this through? The unknown answer must have something to do with Queen's Park. The provincial government has an obvious, oft-stated desire to see the project go ahead—to keep jobs in Ontario, to keep the ONR afloat, to reward its friends. One can only conclude that Mayor Mel is doing its bidding.[17]

Amidst the chaos of the debate, however, Councillor David Miller slipped a poison pill into the deal. Liability had always been the anchor dragging the project back. If something went wrong at the site, Rail Cycle North was only responsible for covering the first $30 million in liability, while Toronto was on the hook for the rest. Without Lastman realizing it, Miller managed to cut Toronto loose from the frightening what-ifs that had plagued the Adams Mine from day one. He amended the contract so that Rail Cycle North was obligated to assume all liability for any future problems with the dump.[18]

Lastman's team hadn't noticed this dramatic amendment as it was pushed forward. But then, Lastman made the surprising announcement that he was supporting the amendment. He declared that the deal was dead unless Rail Cycle North dropped its demand that the city be liable for any "unavoidable costs" or liability from operating the Adams Mine. The original political Bad Boy was digging an escape tunnel from the collapsing political edifice.

Not with a Bang

The vote finally came down on Wednesday, October 11, after what was likely the ugliest day in the history of Toronto Council. Lastman's gang managed to hold together as police cleared the council chamber by force. The images of cops dragging out protesters were flashed on news shows across the country. By mid-afternoon, Case Ootes was ready for the final vote. At 3:45 p.m., the vote came down 32–24 in favour of the Adams Mine dump. There was a disturbing stillness as the vote was read out. It was as if everyone was holding their breath, wondering what was to come next.

This should have been Gordon McGuinty's moment of triumph. But *The Globe and Mail* noted that he looked glum and dispirited. Mayor Lastman's mood was equally dark. The victors looked like they had been badly beaten, while the losers seemed resolute and unbowed. With the vote complete, Chief McBride stood up, hugged Councillor Layton, and then stepped out into the wall of cameras. Although her tone was measured, her words were incendiary: "Toronto has just declared war on northerners. This will make Oka look like a Sunday picnic. After I leave Toronto I will go home and protect our land in any way I can. If I have to give my life for it, I will."[19]

Chief Carol McBride with the Council of Timiskaming First Nation declare their Aboriginal title to the Adams Mine site following the collapse of the Toronto deal. November 2000.

The media pushed her for a response to having lost the vote at city hall. She replied, simply, "It looks like we're going all the way."

A reporter immediately demanded she explain what "going all the way" meant. Pierre Belanger, who was at her side, turned to the reporter. "We want to ask you, how far are *you* willing to go? Are you willing to bring the army to move onto the land of Native people and onto the land of Northern Ontario? How about it?"[20]

This wasn't how it was supposed to go. The city won, the protesters lost. The losing side was supposed to sullenly accept defeat. This was how the political game was played. But once again, Timiskaming hadn't come to play the game. *The Globe and Mail* ran a huge headline

"THE CITY DECLARES WAR." People waited nervously for the next move.

The coming week was a very long one. At Timiskaming First Nation, serious discussions were under way with federal officials about funding for an upcoming federal environmental assessment to override the council decision. Prime Minister Chrétien was a month away from a premature election. The canny leader was looking for another easy romp over the weak Reform Party. But with the growing certainty of a conflict between the rural north and the urban south, the Adams Mine appeared as a political sinkhole. Jean Chrétien wanted this issue off the table. Some political insiders told us they thought the Liberals would use the federal EA to show Lastman that he if didn't deep-six this political nightmare, the federal government would do it for him.

On the Adams Mine Road, the weather turned increasingly cold. A sparse camp of volunteers maintained watch. Retirees Joe Milroy and Shirley Dorsey watched over the camp. The northern organizers used the week to catch their breath, knowing the next phase would be much more difficult. Some volunteers began to prepare for a winter occupation of the mine site itself.

And yet, even as protesters in the north prepared for the escalation of conflict, Terry Graves was hearing intelligence that the deal was falling through. Within two days of the Toronto vote, he received a call from a lawyer very closely connected to the Rail Cycle bid. He told us that Toronto was walking on the deal. This information seemed to be contradicted by everything coming out of Toronto. Although Lastman had gone to ground, city officials were adamant that negotiations were ongoing and the deal would be signed on October 20.

Gordon McGuinty was doing everything he could to keep his consortium together. In his book *Trashed*, he states that Miller Waste Systems lawyer Richard Grant assured city officials that Rail Cycle North was ready to waive the clause on unavoidable costs if the city agreed to be flexible with other parts of the contract. This version is contradicted by information we were receiving from Rail Cycle sources, who let us know that their consortium was not at all willing to accept the liability for the controversial site.

McGuinty had been a master of finding backroom boys to keep his dump dream alive, but now he had become politically toxic. The region of Peel walked on the Adams Mine deal by midweek. Toronto was also looking to cut loose as quickly as possible. At noon on Friday, October 20, Alan Cairnes from the *Sun* called me to ask if I could confirm rumours that the deal was indeed dead. Radio silence was emanating from city hall, but the writing was on the wall. We were holding our breath. Just before 5 p.m., city officials confirmed that the Adams Mine project was not going ahead. The city was going to sign a long-term waste deal with Republic Services of Michigan, while promising Torontonians they would establish major new targets to cut down on the waste stream.

The phone lines began ringing across the rural roads of Timiskaming. People were literally dancing in the streets. When *The Toronto Star* called the Adams Mine campaign office for a comment, Linda Miller answered, "We are going to rock tonight like you have never seen before." And rock we did. The backroom of the Grand Boulevard restaurant in Earlton quickly filled with revellers, drunk with excitement and relief. The war had been avoided. The music and the dancing went on into the early hours of the morning.

Jack Layton and the progressive wing of Toronto City Council had scored an immense victory for recycling and waste diversion efforts. With the civic election looming, Mayor Lastman attempted to outdo Layton as the prophet for urban sustainability. He announced that Toronto was going to move towards 60 per cent waste diversion by 2010. Lastman's council supporters were in a fight for their political lives. Anyone with ties to the Adams Mine faced political defeat. It didn't help that McGuinty was still telling the media that the deal could be revived. Lastman was now doing everything he could to cut his councillors loose from the Adams Mine debacle.

As the *National Post* pointed out,

The Adams Mine deal conveniently fell through after the Mayor realized that some of his key council allies were in serious danger of being dumped as a result of their support for the controversial proposal. Faster than you can say, "reduce, reuse, recycle" TO trash was being redirected to Michigan. Supporters of the project are the target of hisses and boos at almost every turn.[21]

When Layton accused the pro–Adams Mine councillors of planning to revive the deal after the election was over, Lastman blew up: "Adams Mine is D-E-D dead!" he told reporters. "I will do everything to make sure it's never reopened. I will not support Adams Mine and I'll go after anyone who tries to open it at council."

What about Kirkland Lake being a willing host for Toronto garbage? "I don't know if they want it or not, but they're not getting it."[22]

In the aftermath of the debacle, *Star* reporter Royson James blamed a "carefully orchestrated propaganda" campaign by northerners that turned an abandoned mine into a lake. To hear James tell it, wily northerners had outschemed the hapless urbanites and derailed the deal.[23]

Pierre Belanger put it more accurately: "They said we were just a bunch of farmers, French Canadians, Quebec residents, and Indians. But we were smarter and feistier than those buggers."[24]

In the end, what derailed the Lastman-Harris garbage train was that they banked its success on the mistaken belief that urban citizens didn't care what happened to their garbage as long as it was out of sight and out of mind. But Torontonians showed City Council that they did care about environmental issues and were willing to punish politicians at the polls who didn't support a more sustainable waste disposal and reduction plan. The days when big cities would search for a single mega-landfill solution were over. The age of waste diversion and recycling was dawning.

6

Battle on the 401

2001–2002

Gordon McGuinty is confident Toronto will eventually return to the
Adams Mine option. "You should be asking the Ontario government.
Are they going to let this happen [shipping Toronto waste to Michigan]?"
McGuinty says he is working behind the scenes but wouldn't elaborate.

— *Northern Daily News*, January 5, 2001

Mayor Mel Lastman says he isn't a puppet of the Province. But these
days Premier Mike Harris is clearly jerking his strings. Harris must
have smelled blood . . . because he is toying with the mayor—and
Toronto—like an alligator rolling prey before drowning it.

— *The Toronto Star*, February 10, 2001

The Alligator and the Prey

NOTHING EVER HAPPENS in Canada in the first week of January. It's like the nation takes a sleepy pause before readjust-
ing to the slow, uphill grind of another year. But as the clock
counted in 2001, both supporters and opponents of the Adams Mine hit
the ground running. This was a fight to the finish, and Mayor Lastman's
D-E-D pronouncements meant little to either side.

In the wee hours of January 4, 2001, Gordon McGuinty sat down at his computer and mapped out the steps needed to put his project back on track. To succeed, he needed to derail the Republic Services contract as quickly as possible. This was a tall order. Toronto city councillors who had survived the October vote and the subsequent election saw the Adams Mine as political anathema. The city hall doors that had always been open to McGuinty were firmly shut. In early January, Councillor Michael Walker brought forward a motion calling on the city to permanently reject the Adams Mine. The vote passed by a large margin.

Without the Toronto contract, the Adams Mine was history. The Toronto contract was the only contract large enough to justify the massive upfront investment costs required to build the pumping system. To find a way of forcing Toronto back to the table, McGuinty looked to his old buddy Mike Harris. Premier Harris was still a big supporter of the Adams Mine. McGuinty assembled his old gang—Rob Power, Blake Wallace, and Kirkland Lake's ex-mayor Joe Mavrinac—to get the Adams Mine landfill proposal off life-support. The plan was both desperate and audacious. On January 4, he laid it out to Rob Power in an e-mail entitled "Update on Harris from Blake Wallace."

Wallace had always played the role of go-between for Harris and McGuinty. According to McGuinty, Wallace reported the good news that "Harris is pissed"—both at the waste going to Michigan and at "Lastman for putting everybody in this situation."[1]

But it wasn't enough to rely on the anger of Mike Harris. Intervening in a billion-dollar contract between the city of Toronto and a major waste corporation would create numerous political and legal headaches. And so, according to the e-mail, Wallace had taken on the task of finding the best method of making such a coup legal. To pull it off, they would need the support of the Ministry of Environment. Wallace apparently discussed the options with senior bureaucrat Mary Hennessy at the Policy Approvals Branch. McGuinty had faith in Hennessy. In his memoirs, he described her as having a "positive influence" for moving the Adams Mine forward.

The discussion focused on finding the appropriate trigger mechanism to allow the ministry to step in and order a full environmental assessment on the Toronto waste being shipped to the United States. According to the January 4 note, Hennessy apparently agreed that an EA was possible, but the government first needed to establish a credible regulatory change that would justify provincial intervention. In his brief to Power, McGuinty wrote, "Blake [Wallace] says that if a format for EA of Toronto process is available we should make it available."

HighGrader Magazine contacted Mary Hennessy to ask her about whether this discussion took place. She confirmed that a "trigger" would be needed to bring in a provincial EA on the Michigan-bound waste.

"There is nothing in the Act that says how this would work, what municipalities it would apply to and how it would actually be triggered," she stated. She denied talking with anyone directly involved in the Adams Mine project, but when pushed about the contents of the e-mail she confirmed that a discussion had taken place. "I was called and asked how it [the trigger] would work and I basically confirmed what your notes say that it [the means to call an EA] is in the Act."[2]

Hennessy went on to say the Ministry of Environment had not taken any steps to activate this trigger. Ever the optimist, McGuinty set out to provide the ministry with some ideas. "Make it real simple. No [EA] designation if landfill is to take place in Ontario. Designation will only take place if waste is to be shipped out of the province, and is in excess of 50,000 tonnes per year for more than five years. This should pose no hardship on any municipality."[3]

No municipality, that is, other than the city of Toronto. If Toronto was forced to undertake a full EA on waste being shipped to another jurisdiction, it could go a long way to putting the Rail Cycle deal back on the table. Thus McGuinty's e-mail laid out a plan that would allow a garbage promoter from North Bay to rewrite Ontario environmental law in order to take out a rival.

McGuinty followed up with a direct pitch to John Weir, the number two man in the Harris cabinet (underneath top operative Guy Giorno). In the faxed cover letter, McGuinty offered a pro–Rail Cycle report as ammunition for the premier to intervene: "the Province can use this report as justification that Lastman has opted for a USA solution. . . . [that will] cause Republic to hold Toronto ransom. Trust this will be of assistance."[4]

Such a fax could easily have been written off as a desperate long shot by a gambler with nothing to lose. But as we shall see later on, Weir had already been given his marching orders from the premier to go to bat for the Adams Mine. Harris was a political ally of Republican governor John Engler of Michigan. If Engler played ball, then McGuinty's new scheme might just have a chance.

Dump opponents were also working feverishly in the first week of 2001. It didn't matter that Toronto was going ahead with its contract with Republic; we'd seen this movie before. We knew our enemy and we knew that whenever Gordon McGuinty's back was to the wall, he went on the offensive.

Notre remained the driving force in the Rail Cycle North consortium. To keep his partners—particularly CWS—onside, McGuinty needed a new plan to get the Adams Mine back on the table. By moving the pressure to the communities along the Highway 401 corridor, he hoped for a backlash to trucking waste to Michigan that could influence the premier to step in and override Toronto Council.

The fact that we had a copy of McGuinty's secret e-mail plan soon after it was written, however, showed how far we had come as a grassroots resistance movement. We had succeeded in 2000 by using mass marches and rallies to push back against a clear target—the public garbage vote at city hall. Since people were fighting for their own backyard, it was possible to bring maximum pressure to bear. This was a new fight in which it would be harder to bring our natural strengths of people power to bear. We were determined to keep our standing volunteer force active, but to hold our own and stay ahead of Notre Development, we recognized the need to establish extensive political and intelligence contacts.

McGuinty always relied on the small gang of corporate lawyers and Tory insiders. We studied his team and drew charts linking all the players. The connections were put together in a document released to the media called the "Adams Family." It laid out financial and political interplay in this Rubik's cube of greed.

The 2000 campaign had been carried forward on the charismatic leadership of Carol McBride and Pierre Belanger. In this new phase of the battle, I found myself taking on a greater role working alongside Terry Graves. Graves had an astounding network of intelligence. He made it his business to know all the players in the ugly world of garbage. In this cut-throat industry, he tapped the enemies and competitors of Notre for every piece of information on where and how the Notre team was moving.

As for me, I had burned my bridges as a working journalist in the media. *HighGrader Magazine* was still running as a bimonthly publication, but my work on the Adams Mine blockade had lost me badly needed work with both CBC and TVO's Studio 2. Fortunately, Timiskaming First Nation hired me to handle political and research files for their community. This helped pay the bills while I spent the rest of my time increasingly absorbed in tracking the movements of the Notre crew.

Exposing their backroom manoeuvrings required judicious strategizing. As far as most of the media were concerned, Adams Mine was a dead issue. It was essential to provide the media with ironclad information and then find appropriate moments to launch public action. If the timing was off or the information unverifiable, we would be written off as having no credibility. We built careful links with journalists like Kate Harries at *The Toronto Star* and John Nichols at *Maclean's*. In a February 2001 article, Nichols outlined the backroom efforts to put the Adams Mine back in play.

> Behind the scenes maneuvering has continued to get Adams Mine back on the table. . . . Harris has been strident—and furious—at Lastman for letting the deal die. Harris is a friend of North Bay contractor Gordon McGuinty. He is also friends with at least two of the investors, Peter Minogue and his wife Barbara, who was his personal campaign manager. . . . The Harris government is considering taking responsibility for garbage disposal away from Toronto—raising the possibility of Queen's Park reopening the Adams Mine deal. And with Harris angry, the mayor may be paying a price: the city wanted provincial help with its current $305 million shortfall, but talks broke off last week, with Lastman saying he'd have to freeze wages, sell off excess property and raise taxes.[5]

The people of Timiskaming certainly didn't think the Adams Mine was dead. One way of keeping this awareness alive was to keep paying rent on a downtown storefront in New Liskeard. The expenses needed to maintain the office weren't all that difficult to cover. Having a visible presence on a downtown street brought in a steady stream of donations to cover the cost of phones, office space, and pamphlets. As well, an open office was a great way to keep people in the loop and remind the region that the battle was far from over.

At the first mass-organizing meeting in late January 2001, hundreds of volunteers came out to be updated on the coming phase of the fight. So many were interested because they had been kept informed and felt part of the larger strategy. The meeting was frank, with an explanation of what was known and potential options for keeping the pressure on Toronto City Council. Even as the Adams Mine Coalition was galvanizing its volunteers, the other side was launching its next attack to once again put pressure on Toronto Council.

The Michigan Letter

My cell phone rang at 4 p.m. on Friday, February 2. When I saw Terry Graves's number, my heart sank. It seemed that whenever there was bad news to deliver, Graves would learn of it late on a Friday afternoon.

This news was as bad as it could get. According to one of Graves's sources, Harris had talked Michigan governor John Engler into intervening in the upcoming Toronto Works Committee meeting (scheduled for February 7). The intervention was to come in the form of an official letter stating that Michigan didn't want Toronto's garbage and calling on the mayor to revisit the Adams Mine. But this was just the first part of the plan to rock the Works Committee meeting. A group of irate mayors from along the Highway 401 corridor were being organized to demand an end to the 180-plus waste trucks a day rolling down the highway to the Windsor-Detroit border crossing.

The source told us that the plan had actually been cooked up in the premier's office. Further, Harris had personally seconded Joe Mavrinac with the job of "stirring things up" and creating some political "noise" among the mayors along the 401.[6] We were glad to receive this political intelligence, but proving it to the media might not be an easy thing to do.

Thanks to political contacts in Michigan, Graves had a copy of the letter on February 3, even though the letter was dated February 6, 2001. The big question, though, was what to do with this information. A number of the key organizers spent a tense Saturday morning at Graves's house in Haileybury, drinking coffee and going through various scenarios. What were we going to do with a letter that could push Toronto Council into rethinking its position? How could we publicly accuse Harris of trying to initiate a backlash on the 401 without looking like nutters? The only thing we knew for certain was that if we sat still, we were going to be rolled over. So even though the letter could be damaging to us, we were determined to be the ones to release it.

On Monday, February 5, Graves released the Engler letter at a press conference at Queen's Park. He then laid out the evidence we had gathered about Harris's backroom machinations to force the Toronto Works Committee to reopen the Adams Mine bid. To provincial media, the accusations seemed the stuff of conspiracy theory.

"What evidence do you have to suggest Premier Mike is ordering mayors to stir up trouble on the 401?" they demanded. "Are you seriously suggesting that the governor of Michigan is being manipulated to help a North Bay businessman regain a contract?"

These were tough questions, and they were fair. After the press conference ended, it felt as if we had to mop up our own blood. However, it wasn't possible to accurately gauge the media's response until the papers hit the streets the following morning. When they came out, their headlines nailed the other side in big, bold headlines: "TORIES HELP MICHIGAN IN GARBAGE SITE APPEAL — GOVERNOR'S LETTER TO LASTMAN GOT INPUT FROM STAFF IN PREMIER'S OFFICE."

What caused the turnaround? This was the age before Twitter, when the media were built around the twice-a-day news cycle. Thus journalists had time to thoroughly double-check our claims. And given Mike Harris's track record of intervention on the Adams Mine, there was enough plausibility to make our claims worth researching. So just to be on the safe side, they decided to make some calls. And when they made them, they hit political pay dirt. Staff in the governor's office were more than forthcoming in discussing the political interference they had received from Queen's Park. In fact, Engler's press secretary, John Truscott, confirmed that Harris's office helped with the actual wording of the letter.[7]

When the media began calling mayors on the 401 corridor, Sarnia mayor Mike Bradley confirmed that a campaign was under way to organize resistance along the trucking route for the Republic contract. He told *The Toronto Star* that he'd kept notes of telephone conversations that he had with Joe Mavrinac about the Adams Mine and confirmed Premier

Harris's instructions to "stir things up" in order to get the "decision to Michigan reversed."

According to Bradley, the first meeting between Mavrinac and Harris to lay out this strategy took place at a Conservative Party fundraiser shortly after the Adams Mine deal fell apart in October. The second meeting was held in December at Harris's constituency office in North Bay. Mavrinac was given instructions to create a backlash to the Republic deal on the 401 in order to give Harris a reason to step in and annul the Toronto deal. Mayor Bradley was blunt. "They are trying to manipulate us and others to get Adams Mine back on the table."[8]

In releasing the letter a day ahead of time, we had thrown the Notre game plan out the window. They immediately went to ground. Under intense media scrutiny, the Toronto Works Committee sat down to discuss the details of the Republic deal. Works chair Betty Disero, who had previously supported the Adams Mine, told media in no uncertain terms that the Adams Mine option was not being resurrected.

Even Mayor Lastman seemed to gather new fortitude in his willingness to stand up to the bully premier.

> We have a contract with Michigan and the garbage will go to Michigan. They can't break the contract. The Adams Mine is dead. There will be no garbage going to Adams Mine as long as I am Mayor. If the Province wants to pay the cost, let them pay. But the Province is not running Toronto. There is in no way Harris is going to run this city. Everything he's touched has turned to crap.[9]

In early March 2001, *The Toronto Star* provided a clearer picture of the machinations in Michigan. They reported that lawyer Bill Danhof, of Michigan law firm Miller, Canfield, Paddock and Stone, had been hired by unknown persons interested in restarting the Adams Mine process through pressure in Michigan. The lawyer had advised Engler's top policy adviser Dennis Schornack that the "Governor needed to stop Toronto garbage before the city entered the next stage of the contract and filed its nine-month 'intent to ship' notice."[10]

As well, Danhof offered the governor's office the contact information for Harris aide John Weir, and suggested they call Weir for help. Danhof refused to tell media whom he was working for, but he did admit that Weir's phone number was supplied to him "from my client."

Shornack confirmed the conversation with the *Star*. "The lawyer [Danhof] suggested that our office could make a difference and keep Toronto's garbage out of Michigan. It was a chance to tighten the screws."[11]

Even Michigan environmental groups were suspicious of Engler's sudden desire to make Michigan free of Canadian waste. Engler, a right-wing Republican, had been promoting the state as a waste dumping site for years. "This is why [Premier] Harris' involvement makes this so interesting," said Jeff Surfus of the Michigan group No Waste. "We have been trying to get Engler interested in and active in this issue since 1997. We just got no response whatsoever. All of a sudden, one month ago, he starts making these noises. That's what makes this so fishy."[12]

For Harris, his close relation with the Adams Mine deal was causing serious damage to his political credibility. Newspaper articles repeatedly mentioned his personal friendship with mine investors and the North Bay gang pushing the deal. Behind the scenes, some key Conservative insiders reached out to Terry Graves to see if we could find common ground for getting Harris away from the train wreck that was the Adams Mine.

The political unease within the government was growing. An insider told *HighGrader Magazine* that Harris's connection to the Adams Mine was "political suicide. There is nothing to gain from this and everything to lose. Harris' people know that."

But it was going to take a lot more than bad press to wean Mike Harris off the Adams Mine. With the Highway 401 battle won, we quickly turned our attention to numerous other small political fires that were being lit by Notre.

The Big Boss Retires

The people of Michigan had good reason to resent being the waste dumping ground for out-of-state jurisdictions. Having to take Ontario's garbage just made matters worse. Governor Engler's intervention into the Adams Mine issue inadvertently helped kick-start a growing environmental resistance movement in Michigan. NAFTA prevented the governor from shutting the border, but over the next two years, there were continual flare-ups at the border and the ever-present threat that one day Michigan might turn back Toronto's waste for good. As a safety precaution, Republic began seeking out smaller Southern Ontario landfill sites that could be used if Michigan turned back its waste.

This political pressure was helpful to the progressive wing of Toronto Council because it forced the city to maintain its commitment to waste diversion. When it came to dealing with its waste woes, Toronto had no allies. The backlash in Michigan and communities along Highway 401 pushed council towards more ambitious composting and diversion plans. As long as the city could show it was diverting waste streams from the Michigan landfill, it was able to dodge attempts to force a less-enviable solution.

The Michigan border hassles, however, continued to give Notre hope that a backroom deal could be struck. York Region, just north of the city of Toronto, was still solidly in the Adams Mine camp. The Adams Mine promoters continued to try and sign on other Southern Ontario municipalities in the hope of giving the province a reason to step in and push the Toronto contract back into play.

Notre sought a credible launch pad to derail the Toronto deal. If a provincial board took over the planning for Greater Toronto Area trash, that would push Toronto Council to the sidelines.

In February 2001, Don Wanagas of the *National Post* pointed out that the province was considering giving the Greater Toronto Services Board control of the larger GTA garbage issue. According to Wanagas, "The

Province would buy out the contract with Republic and negotiations with Rail Cycle North (RCN), the Ontario company that owns the abandoned Adams Mine near Kirkland Lake, would be restarted."[13]

Board chair Gordon Chong was a former conservative city councillor who had lost his seat to Jack Layton. With the merging of the various boroughs into the larger megacity of Toronto, the Services Board had pretty much lost its reason for carrying on. Chong—who would later reemerge as part of the Rob Ford transition team in 2010—saw the Services Board as an ideal vehicle for taking control of the GTA's garbage contracts.

But Harris wasn't sold. The Conservative government had hammered the New Democrats for intervening in the Toronto waste business through the Interim Waste Authority process in the early 1990s. As much as Harris may have wanted to put the screws to Lastman, such a move involved too many political headaches. The Services Board deal died on the planning table.

The February campaign on the 401 had burned many political fingers, and the odds against Notre were getting greater all the time. In March 2001, Waste Management, Inc., decided that they had had enough and walked on the Adams Mine. Soon after, the bank called in Notre's $300,000 loan. McGuinty was back to being deeply in debt without a dime in his line of credit.[14]

But ever the survivor, McGuinty managed to talk Canada's largest construction company, Aecon, into joining up with Notre. They tried to repaint the project with a "green" hue by renaming the Adams Mine the Enviroganics 2010 initiative. The Enviroganics pitch was first made at a meeting with Works chair Betty Disero in August 2001. Notre offered to build the city a $15 million composting operation at the Adams Mine to divert 25,000 tonnes of waste. City officials saw through the deal immediately. This "green" option represented the diversion of a mere 1.6 per cent of the estimated waste stream and would lock Toronto back into the Adams Mine.

The salesperson for Enviroganics 2010 was the new mayor of Kirkland Lake, Bill Enouy, who had defeated his rival Richard Denton in the 2000 election. He described the compost operation as a "carrot" Toronto couldn't afford to ignore.[15] But the city was in no mood to play. Disero told the *Sun* that a rebirth of the Adams Mine was not in the cards. "I'd prefer not to discuss it again because it is so politically hot . . . it's not productive for council to discuss it."[16]

When Enouy attempted to sell the plan to the Toronto Works Committee, he found himself on hostile ground. "They told me I couldn't mention Adams Mine or Kirkland Lake," he said to local media. "Every time I went to open my mouth, the lady [Councillor Jane Pitfield] said, 'Don't go there. Don't say that.' It was totally rude. . . . We haven't even received a letter back from them that states they have received our proposal. They don't even have the decency to do that."[17]

The Toronto Sun speculated that it was simply because Adams Mine was "the word that turns Toronto Council to jelly."[18]

The city rejected the Enviroganics pitch and voted 40–1 to support the ambitious "green torpedo" organic diversion plan that had been promoted by the Toronto Environmental Alliance. It set out to achieve 60 per cent curbside diversion in five years. "This is a huge victory," said Toronto environmentalist Gord Perks. "It shows that when citizens of Toronto make their voices heard and heard and heard, eventually they will get listened to."

As Notre was getting pounded yet again, word came down that the company was about to lose its number one ally. In October 2001, Premier Harris announced he was leaving politics. Always one to see the advantage in a down situation, McGuinty looked to Harris to provide a going-away present. McGuinty writes: "With Harris not seeking re-election, all the political elements were in place. He would be gone from politics while the review played itself out and he would be able to say he protected Ontario's interests. . . . It should have been a non-issue."[19]

But Harris was getting tired of McGuinty's schemes. Despite a last-minute flurry of pressure to get him to force the Adams Mine through, Harris stopped taking Notre's calls and then stepped off into the political sunset. With Harris suddenly gone, Notre's team was desperate to find another champion in the remaining Conservative cabinet. The year ended with a mad scramble to get Environment Minister Chris Hodgson to intervene in the Toronto Council vote and order the city to turn its waste decision-making authority over to a yet-to-be-formed regional body.

On November 29, *The Globe and Mail* reported Hodgson's willingness to step into the fray, claiming he had been asked by Gordon Chong to intervene. The news caused major political blowback for the low-key Ernie Eves, who was looking to replace Harris as premier.

In early December, we decided to once again take the fight to our political enemies. John Vanthof, Terry Graves, and I held a press conference at the King Street bank tower in Toronto where Eves was working in the private sector. Eves was preparing a run for the premier's job and was doing his best to distance himself from Harris's polarizing record. He certainly didn't want to be dragged into the Adams Mine morass. We held a press conference outside Eves's office and demanded he explain whether or not he would go along with the public musings of Hodgson and Chong to support reopening Adams Mine.

Some in the media dutifully reported on the protest. Others clearly thought we were crazy. But we had developed very thick skins, and our strategy was to hammer anyone who touched the file. In his memoirs, McGuinty grudgingly admits that we were "smart" to target Eves as he was attempting to define himself apart from Harris. Minister Hodgson felt the heat as well. On December 4 he announced he would not intervene in the Toronto contract in any way. The next day, Toronto Council voted to finalize the terms of the Republic deal.

We attended the Toronto vote and when it was done, Terry Graves walked right into the heart of the council and presented Mayor Lastman with a framed Adams Mine poster. Lastman was clearly sick of us, but ever the politician, he smiled for a photograph shaking hands with Graves.

McGuinty didn't have anything to smile about. The Adams Mine backers felt that Harris had walked away on them. He failed to deliver a billion-dollar going-away present to the investors. From that point on, there was bad blood between McGuinty and Harris.

In his memoirs, McGuinty describes finally speaking with Harris by phone on October 1, 2009. It was the first time they had talked in years and the way McGuinty tells it, Harris wasn't pleased. "The call did not begin well, and I was a little shocked. Mike said he was pissed off at me; he had heard that I had been bad-mouthing him over the past two years, and he almost didn't bother to call. I replied that I had never bad-mouthed him."

McGuinty told Harris he didn't mean anything personal by his comments. Nonetheless, he needed to ask, why hadn't Harris overturned the Michigan contract as he was leaving office?

"Why should I have bailed Lastman out of his mess? If Toronto wants to be stupid . . . it's their problem," he replied. "No one was asking me for a review [of the Toronto contract], and my legal advice was I couldn't do it."[20]

McGuinty wasn't one to be deterred by the legal limits imposed on the office of the premier. "The statement was totally wrong—" writes McGuinty in his memoirs "—the evidence was overwhelming—but Mike skated around the issue and said he couldn't remember everything." McGuinty goes on to diss Harris: "[He] didn't give a damn about developing an in-Ontario solution . . . nor did he care about the economy of the north."[21]

Harris had tarnished his political reputation by advocating his golfing buddy's scheme. But in the end, he didn't get a word of thanks. No wonder Harris was pissed.

7

The Sacrifice Zone
1999–2002

The worst oil spill in history was the best boost to business
John Bennett ever had. . . . "Every time there is a major disaster
like this, there's a surge in business," says Bennett.
— *The Vancouver Sun*, December 30, 1989

In licensing these incineration operations, the government is
creating zones of sacrifice. I'm not just talking about people getting
sick. I've seen them die. If the wind would blow the smoke towards
the school on a Monday you'd see children being at home sick on
Tuesday and Wednesday. The schools near incinerators had the
highest absentee rates in the district. I met a lot of these
children. I've seen them die of leukemia, brain
cancer, and a host of other disorders.

— DR. NEIL CARMAN, former incinerator inspector for
the State of Texas, New Liskeard, May 15, 2002

Voyage of the Wan He

I T WAS NEVER just about the Adams Mine. Local economic development planners were banking on the premise that once the megalandfill was established, other waste businesses could be enticed into the area. Kirkland Lake was actively recruiting companies to set up in what they were calling the environmental solutions capital of North America. Waste companies that may have been unwelcome anywhere else now had a new home. The first company to take up the offer was Trans-Cycle Industries (TCI) of Pell City, Alabama. In late 1998, they set up a recycling plant for PCBs (polychlorinated biphenyl) in a newly created industrial park in Kirkland Lake. Local anti-dump activists had been suspicious of the potential impact of this PCB plant, but with so much energy focused on fighting on the Adams Mine, TCI managed to pass under the radar.

All that changed in early 2000 when the U.S. army publication *Stars and Stripes* casually mentioned that a ship, the *Wan He*, was headed to Canada with a cargo of ninety thousand kilos of PCB-contaminated waste. The waste was in the form of used transformers and other contaminated metals from a U.S. Army Base at Sagami, Japan. International toxic waste NGOs began to sound the alarm bells. But none of them knew where this mysterious ship's cargo was headed.

It soon became known that the contract was held by TCI. The only problem was that TCI, which ran two plants in the United States (New York and Alabama), was forbidden by United States law to import PCB materials. As for its newly opened plant in Kirkland Lake, it didn't have a licence to import international toxic waste. Even stranger was the fact that since coming to Kirkland Lake, the company had made no mention of having any intention of looking to international waste for source materials. TCI president David Laskin had sold the plant to locals on the promise of being a part of a "regional" solution for PCB waste from old mines and mills.

"We were dying for any new business at all," recalls one local businessman. "They [TCI] came in and were very sophisticated. We went down and saw their operation in Alabama. We were impressed by their pitch. But I don't remember any talk about the plant taking waste from other jurisdictions. I was under the impression they were going to serve regional needs."[1]

TCI promised sixty-eight local jobs at a state-of-the-art facility, the largest of its kind in North America. It was music to the ears of local politicians. In the wake of the TCI announcement, a tire recycling/burning plant (Unisphere Waste Conversion) also expressed interest in coming to town. As well, Bennett Environmental stated its intention to build a PCB incinerator.

Kirkland Lake was desperate for jobs. The historic Macassa gold mine had shut down following a brutal rock burst (cave-in) underground. As well, the once-rich Kerr-Addison Mine had closed in neighbouring Virginiatown. Little wonder that the appearance of TCI drew immediate support from regional federal and provincial economic development agencies. The federal government kicked in a $1.25 million forgivable loan through the Canada Jobs Fund. A regional funding agency gave them another $500,000.[2]

But as international media began tracking the voyage of the *Wan He*, the glow was quickly coming off TCI. The question was whether or not TCI had set up in Kirkland Lake in the hope of securing contracts that were beyond the reach of its U.S. operations. It took a lot of nerve to attempt to import toxic contaminants through an international port without a licence. But given the record of the Harris government, it is easy to see why the company may have thought it had arrived in a toxic promised land.

Until 1997, the Canada-U.S. border was firmly closed to the trade in PCBs. But in 1997, the feds, fearing potential NAFTA retaliation, quietly backed away from their closed-door stance. So far, no company had actually tested the grey waters surrounding NAFTA and toxic imports. The federal move came as the Harris government signalled an open-door policy on toxic waste.[3] Ontario is by far the largest producer of hazardous waste in Canada and had been deemed the second-worst polluter in all of North America by the Committee for Environmental Cooperation.

Under the Harris Conservatives, hazardous waste shipments from the United States into Ontario skyrocketed. In 1993, hazardous waste imports stood at 85,000 tonnes. Within four years, that total had risen almost three times to 230,000 tonnes.

Mark Winfield of the Canadian Institute for Environmental Law and Policy stated that TCI's provocative move was a direct result of Mike Harris's new "open for waste business" policy. "The Province has opened the gates. They've given the green light to any hazardous waste imports to Ontario. We are certainly becoming a continental dumping ground."

Winfield said that as U.S. toxic waste laws were becoming stricter, Ontario was turning into a destination of choice for dumping. "The signal from the Province is that anything will get approved. The Ministry of Environment has lost its ability to regulate this because they've lost about a third of their staff and 40% of their budget. Ontario is a very attractive place to dispose of wastes cheaply."[4]

As the *Wan He* slowly moved across the ocean, it drew increasing attention. In response to the growing media scrutiny, TCI owner David Laskin went to ground. Working as a journalist for *HighGrader Magazine* (and for the online publication *Straight Goods*), I managed to track down company lawyer Michael Zarin at his office in Westchester, New York. Zarin tried to shrug off the fact that they didn't actually have a licence for international imports.

"You know, frankly, we thought we did [fill out an application for international approval]. But the MOE claimed this wasn't clear on our original application. This is why we are going back now to amend it."[5]

But the Ministry of Environment, which had been so discredited on the Adams Mine fight, was not willing to play chump to this outfit from Alabama. Ian Parrott, of the MOE Approvals Branch, told *HighGrader Magazine* there was no mix-up in approvals. "I can't tell you what they thought they were applying for but I can tell you what they did apply for, and what they were approved for, and that was Canada."

Zarin said the decision to illegally import ninety thousand kilos of toxic waste from Japan was no big deal. "It's not as if there is going to be any new environmental impact from amending our application. The environment is not aware of whether you are treating PCBS from Ontario or from Mexico."[6]

International toxic waste campaigners didn't share Zarin's *que sera, sera* attitude. Greenpeace threatened to block access to harbours on the West Coast. Members of the Basel Action Network, an NGO monitoring the international traffic in toxic waste, denounced TCI's efforts as a provocation that would unleash a whole new level of international trade in PCBS. They were particularly concerned that it would undermine the Basel Convention, which had been signed by 130 countries to stop the trade of toxic waste into countries with lower standards. If TCI succeeded in this first shipment from Japan, it would open up opportunities for importing waste from other U.S. military bases in Guam, Japan, and Korea.

Jim Puckett, spokesperson for the Basel Action Network, described TCI's claim that it was pursuing a "minor" amendment as "outrageous." According to Puckett, "What they are doing is opening the door from one country to 130 countries. If you throw in all the Basel countries, which have a membership of about 130 countries, there are really very few countries left [that wouldn't be part of TCI's market]. This [amendment] would open their market by magnitudes. It's not a minor issue at all."

He warned Canadians that if the *Wan He* shipment was successful, it would be impossible to stop the flood of more international waste. "The reason TCI is making money is because the metals are contaminated with some of the most hazardous substances on the planet. That's where the money is. I'm sorry, these guys aren't scrap dealers. There is a huge market out there in PCB-contaminated waste. And who is going to stop a successful company from expanding to meet this market?"[7]

By the time the ship drew close to the harbour in Vancouver, both the federal and Ontario governments had been fully drawn into the controversy.

Zarin claimed that the waste products were under fifty parts per million (ppm) of PCBS and thus TCI was under no obligation to tell either level of government of its cargo. Said Zarin, "We don't need a license. We don't need to talk to nobody."[8]

Ontario, however, seemed to disagree. Jeff Chatterton, communications adviser to Ontario's environment minister Dan Newman, was blunt, "We have a company . . . [with a] certificate of approval that explicitly says they cannot accept waste that is generated outside of Canada. The last time I checked, Japan isn't even a border country."[9]

When I called Zarin back, he played the tough guy. "You either misconstrued what they [MOE officials] said or they were talking loosely," said Zarin. "It's going to Kirkland Lake."

With their hand all but forced, the province told TCI it was not allowed to ship the waste to Kirkland Lake, while the federal government stated the ship would be stopped from entering the port in Vancouver. An attempt to divert the ship to the United States was scuttled on April 5, 2000, when the Teamsters announced they would block it from entering the port of Seattle.

Now completely stymied, the ship had no choice but to head back to Japan. With relations already strained with the Japanese, the last thing the U.S. Department of Defense wanted to contemplate was the prospect of a return voyage.

On April 16, 2000, Greenpeace protesters boarded the ship as it entered the Japanese port of Yokohama. The protesters unfurled a large banner reading "United States—Toxic Criminals." The banner summed up the anger in Japan over the large stockpiles of toxic waste stored at U.S. bases.

Blocked from entering Japan, the ship wandered the ocean aimlessly until the U.S. military managed to set up a location to "temporarily" store the waste on Wake Island in the North Pacific. The containers were taken ashore and dumped.[10] It was an international PR disaster for the U.S. military. Politically, there was huge fallout as well. Jim Puckett, writing in *The Seattle Times*, stated that the blockade of the *Wan He* represented a major turning point in handling international waste.

> The current "ship and burn" response to the global problem of POPs (persistent organic pollutants) destruction . . . creates an international shell game where toxic wastes will be shuttled around the world according to the dictates of a free market, seeking out the path of least resistance—the cheapest and dirtiest incinerators and landfills available.[11]

For its part, TCI blamed the feds and the province. Zarin said it was a big mistake on the part of bureaucrats. "It wouldn't be productive to point fingers. Everybody's trying to cover their 'you-know-what.'"[12] Thwarted in its attempt to set up an international waste import business, TCI mused publicly (though it didn't follow through) that it didn't feel welcome in Canada and might consider leaving, despite its significant federal loan.

But the debacle of the *Wan He* woke local people up to the threat posed by an open-door policy on waste. Through contacts with groups like the Basel Action Network, our grassroots team in Timiskaming began to understand the magnitude of the international waste trade. It was clear that unless we shut the door firmly to such schemes, Timiskaming would become a destination of choice for other toxic waste and burning operations.

The Genetic Hand Grenade

Where other people saw disaster, John Bennett saw opportunity. Take the toxic contamination at Monsanto's former PCB plant in Anniston, Alabama. Over the years, Monsanto dumped millions of pounds of PCBs into nearby streams and landfills. The company had invented and marketed polychlorinated biphenyls as a miracle product. The greasy liquid served as a non-flammable insulator used in electrical equipment and transformers. It was often added to paper, glues, and paints. The problem was that

PCBS created a permanent toxic stain on the environment and posed cumulative risks that were magnified on the higher levels of the food chain. No one in the early years knew that PCBS posed a serious threat to human health. No one, that is, but Monsanto.

In 1966, a Monsanto scientist at the Anniston plant dropped twenty-five perfectly healthy fish into the nearby Snow Creek to see what would happen. After ten seconds, the fish were belly up and spitting blood. In four minutes they were all dead. Their skins had been shredded off. But Monsanto didn't tell the workers at the plant. They didn't tell the locals who fished the waters for food. And they didn't tell the children who played in the streams. These unpleasant facts were hidden in internal documents emblazoned with the warning "CONFIDENTIAL: Read and Destroy."[13]

By the dawn of the millennium, Anniston was one of thousands of abandoned sites across North America that were heavily contaminated with PCBS, POPS (persistent organic pollutants), and dioxin. That's where John Bennett stepped in. The affable Englishman had spent years as a chief engineer at Monsanto U.K. After the company was barred from producing PCBS, he got into the business of cleaning up the mess. The problem was, PCBS weren't easy to get rid of. The most obvious solution was to burn them, but doing so opened a toxic Pandora's box. The burning of polychlorinated compounds inevitably creates dioxin and the various sister elements known as dibenzofurans. Even microscopic trace elements can cause miscarriages, genetic damage, and cancers. Once the fingerprint of dioxin has been established on the local environment, it cannot be erased.[14]

Mobile incineration has been one solution for cleaning up PCB sites. Temporary incineration still creates dioxin residues, but given the overall contamination of the site, these trace elements are sometimes considered the lesser of two evils. The problem with mobile burning, however, is that you can't make a lot of money at it. Bennett's solution was to dig up the contaminated soil and truck it across the continent where it could be burned in a much larger permanent incinerator. His big problem was finding a community willing to become the host of North America's most toxic soil.

Bennett had two sales pitches. The first pitch was to investors, where he played up the dangers posed by PCBS and the urgent need to clean them up. Speaking to the *Wall Street Corporate Reporter* he stated, "The chemical [PCBS] enters the water table and then gets into the food chain, which causes serious birth defects and cancers." The upside of this toxic nightmare for investors was that he had cornered a "niche market" in dealing with "dioxin . . . which now, after many years of research, they've discovered is the most toxic element known to man."[15]

Bennett's pitch to locals, however, downplayed the dangers considerably. When I interviewed him for *HighGrader Magazine* in 2000, he said PCBS weren't even linked to cancer. "If you look at the toxicity scale it is not a known carcinogen . . . I don't know why people pick on PCBS of all the things that people can pick on."[16]

Nonetheless, his reassuring sales banter wasn't going very well. His company, Bennett Environmental, tried setting up in British Columbia but was given the toss from Fort St. John, Golden, and Abbotsford before landing in Taylor, where the community was highly divided over the proposal. As the Taylor process bogged down, Bennett looked for other locations. The company was forced to walk away from $371,163 they had shelled out exploring a site in West Virginia, citing permit and land-use problems. He tried and failed to pitch his state-of-the-art technology to citizens worried about PCB contamination of the Housatonic River in Pittsfield, Massachusetts.[17]

Finally, in 1996 Bennett got his foot in the door in the small Quebec town of Saint-Ambroise, by promising to treat soil contaminated with "hydrocarbons"—that is, gasoline. When truckloads of PCB-contaminated soil hit town, the locals freaked. A local grassroots campaign rose up to try and shut the plant down, but with an operating licence in hand, Bennett was firmly entrenched in the region.

Bennett Environmental was keen to get a similar foothold in Kirkland Lake. The town had built a new industrial park on the south side of the community to welcome "environmental solutions." Bennett promised to build the largest incinerator of its kind in North America. It would receive PCB and dioxin-contaminated soils from Mexico, the United States, and across Canada.

Bennett Environmental hit town in 2001–2002. Using a strategy much like Gordon McGuinty's, the company tried to contain the backlash by defining the language of the debate. The word "incinerator" was never used. Instead, they consistently used the phrase "state-of-the-art technology" in describing the "Mark IV thermal oxidizer." It sounded futuristic and safe. The local advertising also painted John Bennett as a genial environmentalist. "Sure John Bennett is a businessman but first and foremost he is an environmentalist," boasted a Bennett promotional pamphlet. The message box then went on to smooth over concerns about toxicity: "We all get bent out of shape about the words dioxins and furans . . . this Grandfather of six cares and so should you."[18]

Bennett was backed by a wave of positive coverage in the media that made it seem as if this "thermal oxidizer" had unlocked the magic code of making money from environmental disasters. Bennett arrived in a region with a well-organized population that was flush with victory over the Adams Mine. As Terry Graves told local media, "Bennett made a major mistake when it assumed it would be dealing with disorganized citizens. Our region has been fighting environmental issues for two decades. People are organized. They are militant and they know how to win."[19]

The first step for opponents was to ensure that Bennett did not define the language of the debate. Once people understood that this space-age oxidizer was in fact an incinerator that burned soil in a stack, it became much easier to begin levelling the terms of the debate.

Nonetheless, the Bennett campaign looked very daunting. The biggest initial problem was battle fatigue. It felt as if the region had been plunged into a never-ending war against predatory waste companies. The Adams Mine battle had sapped people's energy. Many stalwart fighters against the Adams Mine didn't want to start another long, bitter fight. Perhaps, some thought, the fears were overblown.

The Adams Mine Coalition was rebranded as Public Concern Timiskaming (PCT). Our first task was to find a way to deconstruct the pseudo-science behind incineration so that the public would understand the issues and get engaged. Our opponent already had an enormous head start. Even worse, the Ministry of Environment had decided there wasn't even going to be a public EA hearing. This meant a very limited window to develop a coherent strategy that could knock this project out of the game.

The first sparring session came at a public meeting held by the Temiskaming Federation of Agriculture on January 9, 2002, at Northern College in Kirkland Lake. Only 150 people showed up. John Bennett sent his right-hand salesperson, Danny Ponn, to reassure locals. Ponn was a plodding, methodical guy and he brought with him the usual consultant team of "experts."

We had learned our lesson in the Adams Mine battle and weren't going to be bamboozled by the hired-gun consultants. PCT's volunteer researchers had been using the internet to track world-renowned experts in PCBS and incineration. Two of these leading voices were invited to the meeting. Much to everyone's surprise, Paul Connett, an expert in dioxin, and Neil Carman, a former incinerator inspector for the State of Texas—both veterans of waste wars across the United States—agreed to come north. Their presence at the forum threw the Bennett team off their game. These two experts were easily able to debunk the myth of "state-of-the-art" incineration technology.

Dr. Connett was a chippy Brit from St. Lawrence University in Canton, New York. He ridiculed Ponn's attempt to portray the incinerator as a flawless system. "You know what state-of-the-art means? It means the latest experiment with the latest crappy operation," he declared. Connett was as much an activist as an academic, and he knew how to explain the threats posed by burning PCBs and the creation of dioxin elements. "Dioxin is like a genetic hand grenade," he told the audience.

Connett challenged pro-incinerator assertions that the Timiskaming dairy region was at a safe distance from the proposed facility. "In one day a cow puts into its body as much dioxin as a human would breathe in fourteen years and then delivers this dioxin back to humans," he said. "The last place you want to put an incinerator is where you have agriculture. Thirty kilometres is not a long distance from an incinerator. Dioxins travel thousands of kilometres."

Dr. Carman was lower-key in his talk, but he struck an emotional chord with residents when he painted a disturbing picture of how toxic trade was tied to the much larger issue of economic and environmental injustice. Carman explained how poorer regions of the United States are deliberately targeted as sites for incineration. These have-not regions bear the health and social effects of toxic contamination.

"What is the effect on the communities? I saw children with brain cancers, leukemia, children too sick to go to school. The families told me they felt their community had been turned into a sacrifice zone for industry. I met a lot of these children. I went to cemeteries where they are buried. The parents took me out to show me where they were buried—children younger than ten dying from cancers. This is what it means to allow the creation of sacrifice zones," he said.

For people in Timiskaming, Carman's words hit home. Tired though they were of the waste wars, they were not going to let their region become North America's latest sacrifice zone. As the Northern College session drew to a close, volunteers began signing up for the new battle.

Backlash on the Doctors

The sales pitch was certainly impressive. But John Bennett hadn't banked on the country folk in Timiskaming wanting to take a peek under the hood. One the key lessons learned in the Adams Mine fight was to check every claim that was made. Brit Griffin undertook a thorough investigation of Bennett's corporate history. She researched the test burn data from the existing incinerator, talked to communities where Bennett had tried to sell its technology, and studied the financial and corporate statements to seek out inconsistencies.

The company had promised to build a "next generation" incinerator with an efficiency rate of 99.9999 per cent. But the reality is, the benchmark of 99.9999 per cent efficiency in burning isn't an operation norm, it is a minimum standard set by regulators because anything less will pose major health concerns. Incinerators do not monitor the contaminants coming out of the stack. In order to be approved by the Ministry of Environment, operators have to show that it is theoretically possible to reach the benchmark of 99.9999 per cent through a carefully prepared test burn. This test burn would be similar to judging a car's performance the day it is driven off the lot, and not considering the wear and tear on the vehicle over the next ten years. Incinerators operate 24/7 under very trying conditions and are rarely able to replicate the safety standard promised in the Certificate of Approval.[20]

In its corporate filings, Bennett stated it was planning to build this next generation burner with parts from a shut-down dioxin incinerator from Times Beach, Missouri. This used incinerator had been plagued with problems.[21] An article in the *St. Louis Post-Dispatch* pointed out the difficulties of meeting the 99.9999 per cent standard:

The difference between 99.9999 percent and 99.96 percent may seem minuscule, but it could prove monumental. . . . No incinerator has been able to achieve that goal . . . the difference in 99.9999 percent destruction of dioxin and 99.96 percent—the level most often achieved [is that] nearly an ounce of dioxin would escape into the air over St. Louis, compared with 0.0022 of an ounce at the higher destruction rate. And while an ounce may seem to be a tiny amount. . . . The toxicological properties of dioxin are discussed in parts per quadrillion.[22]

Very early in the Bennett campaign, Public Concern Timiskaming reached out to the local opposition group in Saint-Ambroise. The Quebec group provided a clear picture of the problems that had plagued the Saint-Ambroise operation, including numerous unintentional discharges of gases.

Burning soil requires intense heat, which creates inevitable instability for a sealed unit. If any problems are detected, the incinerators rely on trip mechanisms that will immediately flush toxic gases through a vent stack, preventing high-pressure explosions in the burn unit. Unintentional venting happens for numerous reasons, including malfunction, operator error, and power outages, and it can inundate the local environment with a highly toxic brew of dioxin, furan, and PCB contaminants. Such contaminants are not tracked because incinerators are not required to monitor their stack's emissions.[23]

The Saint-Ambroise plant had raised alarm bells with local Quebec Health authorities over the presence of trace elements of dioxin near the plant.[24] It wasn't clear whether the dioxin had been there all along, as Bennett claimed, or was the result of stack ventings and potentially problematic burning cycles at the plant.

And yet, the Saint-Ambroise operation was used by Bennett as an example of the safety that could be expected at the much larger Kirkland Lake operation. For example, the company stated in its EA application that there had been only six upsets (that resulted in the venting of gas into the surrounding environment) at its existing incinerator at Saint-Ambroise. The company also guaranteed that any upsets at the much larger Kirkland Lake facility would be limited to a maximum of one minute.

This claim was wrong. Documents from Quebec obtained under a Freedom of Information request showed there had been numerous upsets, including seven in a six-month period. All of them were much longer than the promised one-minute limit. One upset, on December 29, 2001, lasted a total of fourteen minutes.[25] We publicly challenged the Ministry of Environment on these obvious discrepancies. But EA director Michael Williams stated that this evidence on problems at the Saint-Ambroise facility wasn't admissible. The ministry was prepared to accept Bennett's claims of a near-flawless operation at Saint-Ambroise, but would not accept evidence of accidents that contradicted these claims because the incidents occurred in Quebec and were thus not applicable to an Ontario application.

Ministry spokesperson John Steele said it wasn't fair to compare the two operations, because the Kirkland Lake operation represented a different generation of technology (even though the plan stated that the incinerator would be built with used parts from the Times Beach incinerator). Comparing problems at Saint-Ambroise to the Kirkland Lake operation, according to Steele, would be like "comparing apples and oranges."[26]

The apples and oranges in this case happened to be two incinerators, both called the Mark IV thermal oxidizer. Both were to be built and operated by Bennett and both would burn similar materials. The main difference was that the Kirkland Lake incinerator was to be at least twice the size.

Terry Graves accused the Ministry of Environment of attempting to "squash the accident reports" on Bennett's operations in Quebec. "The whole Bennett EA is based on its supposed clean working history at St. Ambroise. If the upsets and accidents at this plant aren't admissible then none of Bennett's evidence should be admissible."[27]

Another claim made by Bennett was that the Kirkland Lake incinerator would easily meet every guideline laid down by the CCME (Canadian Council of the Ministers of the Environment).[28] But one of the key CCME guidelines was that no hazardous waste incinerator should be sited within 1.5 kilometres of a residential neighbourhood. The proposed

Bennett incinerator (soon to be a neighbour of TCI's PCB cleaning operation) would be a mere 500 metres from a residential street, and within a
kilometre of two grade schools and a daycare.

The proximity to local elementary schools pushed the local medical community into action. On April 10, 2002, ten local doctors in Kirkland Lake issued a statement warning against the effects of the toxic waste
incinerator and its proximity to the grade school:

> PCBs, dioxins, furans and heavy metals are harmful to fetuses, babies and
> children, leading to abortions, genetic malformations, cancers and men-
> tal and behavioral problems. The proposed PCB incinerator of Bennett
> is to be built within a 1.5 km. radius of two elementary schools, a day
> care, a kindergarten and 240 homes. Therefore, be it resolved that we the
> undersigned physicians feel it is not in the public's best interest to have
> the Bennett incinerator built this close to schools.

Doctors enjoy a very special status in small towns, especially in regions
faced with chronic doctor shortages. And yet, within days of their statement, these doctors came under vicious attack from the pro-waste economic and political interests in Kirkland Lake. One particularly vitriolic
local editorial trashed their credibility and sneered at their wealthy privi-
lege. The *Northern Daily News* article, "Doctors Twisted Tales," was over
the top even when compared to the take-no-prisoners approach that had
divided the community during the Adams Mine fight. In response to this
attack, the larger medical community came together in an unprecedented
show of support, with thirty-four Timiskaming doctors signing a public
letter of solidarity with their Kirkland Lake colleagues.

The provincial medical authorities also joined the fight. The Ontario
College of Family Physicians wrote to the Ministry of Environment calling on them to reject the Bennett proposal:

The inevitable contamination of residential, farm and wilderness land with PCBS, dioxins, furans and heavy metals (to name a few) will adversely affect the health of the people, animal life and vegetation. Bennett Environmental Inc. and any other company for that matter, which engages in such actions will be regarded by physicians at large, as having a direct attack on the health of the public, putting at risk children, aged, infirm, pregnant (with emphasis on the fetus) and infants who are breast-fed.[29]

As the Bennett fight waged on, provincial medical authorities were drawn further into the file. They paid for a visit to the community by Chicago-based Dr. Peter Orris, a worldwide expert on dioxin contamination. This high-powered alliance of medical expertise came together as the mobilizing efforts against the campaign moved into increasingly militant action.

But as impressive as this medical solidarity was, the damage in the local medical community had been done. On April 19, 2002, Dr. Marianne Talman announced she was closing her practice and leaving town. Dr. Ted Mitchell was the next to leave. The loss to the community of Kirkland Lake was profound.

After years of fighting garbage and now toxic incineration, people began to sense what it means to live in a sacrifice zone. New doctors weren't interested in taking the place of the family practitioners who had quit town. It seemed as if many local residents were wrestling with whether or not to abandon a region they loved. Barb Biederman-Bukowski sold her house and moved to North Bay. Norm MacDonald and his wife, Brenda, sold their dream home on Round Lake and moved to South Timiskaming. Hugh Reynolds, who had moved north to enjoy his retirement, packed his bags as well. Farm leaders John and Fran Nychuk also moved.

The Public Concern Timiskaming campaign was now in full battle mode against the incinerator, but the wear and tear on the region was becoming obvious. No one wanted to think of what would happen if the campaign failed.

Crashing the King Eddie

John Bennett was a rising star in the business press. Bennett Environmental had been mired among the small-time stock wannabes but was now beginning to look like the next big thing. Speaking to the *Wall Street Transcript*, John Bennett was bullish. "Just look at the news release that I put out. You'll see what our backlog is, you'll see what our earnings are.... This is not a flyer, I think it's a very solid investment, and I think in a few years you are going to look at a $30–$40 stock."[30]

The buzz was tied to Bennett's plan to build the new incinerator in Kirkland Lake. Investors from across North America were invited to the annual shareholders' meeting set for Toronto's King Edward Hotel on May 9, 2002. This was to be investors' chance to see if the plan lived up to the hype. Little did they know that Public Concern Timiskaming had also decided to pay a visit to the King Eddie.

The decision to take the fight to the shareholders' meeting was very much in line with the lessons learned in the Adams Mine fight. We didn't really have a full plan of how we were going to crash the party, but we were determined to make as big a splash as possible. In a statement issued by Public Concern Timiskaming, Terry Graves put the Bennett shareholders on notice.

> We will do what is necessary to ensure this proposal does not go ahead. There will be no accommodation, no willingness to come to terms with this project somewhere down the road. This is the message we bring to Bennett and their shareholders today. From this point on, your company and your investors are on notice. This project will be beaten.[31]

The Toronto strike team headed out early in the morning of May 9, 2002. There were two vans of volunteers and one flatbed trailer carrying the mascot Mel the Moose. For the PCB fight, Mel had been refashioned with a white vinyl protective suit with gas mask. The flatbed was decked

Saugeen Drummers of Timiskaming First Nation protest outside the King Edward Hotel during Bennett shareholder meeting. May 9, 2002.

out with large signs declaring "NO TOXIC WASTE—RESPECT THE NORTH." Accompanying us on the trip were the Saugeen powwow drummers of Timiskaming First Nation.

It rained hard all day. Arriving early, the drummers headed over to Queen Street West so that they could visit the famous MuchMusic Speakers' Corner. For the price of a loonie, Wayne MacKenzie, Rodney Stanger, and their fellow singers squeezed into the filming booth, took out their hand drums, and began to chant.

The music filled the street. Passersby stopped and gathered around. A woman came through the crowd and asked me why we were there. She had a strong Dublin accent and was, perhaps, a little unbalanced. When I explained to her about our fight against the incinerator, she suddenly proclaimed, "St. Michael the Archangel has told me he is giving his blessing upon you and your group today." With that she slipped back into the crowd.

We climbed into the vehicles and the gloomy, hard rain ended immediately. The sun came out as we drove over to the King Edward Hotel on King Street. Having beat the rain, a second seemingly impossible obstacle appeared; it was rush hour and the hotel wasn't likely to allow a large trailer with protesters to block the street and cause trouble for the wealthy patrons. Nonetheless, Ambrose Raftis, who was driving the truck and trailer, walked up to the doorman and explained why we were there. Much to our shock, hotel staff cleared a path for our large trailer with Mel the Moose on the back. We were set up right in front of the historic hotel!

The Bennett investors began to arrive at 4 p.m. to the defiant chants of the Saugeen Drummers. The music echoed off the walls of the office towers. People came out of the nearby buildings to watch. Angry investors had to walk the gauntlet through northern protesters. MPP Gilles Bisson showed up from Queen's Park and gave a wonderful tirade from a microphone set up on the back of the truck.

We then sent our ultimate secret weapon into the meeting—retired teacher Alex Melaschenko, who had a lame leg from a childhood spent in a Nazi labour camp in Ukraine. He wasn't the kind who liked to be pushed around, and he was furious at the predatory waste plans that kept popping up in his region. Melaschenko had purchased one share in the company and had every right to be there. From the beginning of the meeting, he openly challenged John Bennett and questioned his glib promises. Angry investors attempted to shut him down, but he was fearless. By the end of the meeting, Bennett was so thrown off he ended up in an all-out argument with Melaschenko.

This was supposed to be a day of positive promotion for the Bennett plan. Instead, it was a public relations debacle. When the investors began leaving the building, it was clear that many didn't want to have anything to do with us or, for that matter, with the Bennett plan. PCT's job was done.

Before leaving, I went up to thank the hotel's head of security for his professionalism. I still couldn't get over the fact that they had allowed us to hold the demonstration right in front of the hotel.

"We know all about you guys," he confided. "We knew you were coming, and so we decided to check you guys out. In our book, you're fighting the good fight. Good luck."

Score two for Michael the Archangel. Nil for the Bennett incinerator.

The Parmalat Bombshell

As Bennett struggled to maintain confidence with its investors, rallies of ever-increasing size were held in Timiskaming. The campaign extended its reach through a growing network of activists in neighbouring Abitibi-Témiscamingue. On April 12, 2000, breastfeeding mothers staged a protest march outside the Agence régionale de la santé in Rouyn-Noranda, Quebec.

Quebec environmental activist Lise Chartrand led the march. "Mothers bear the greatest risk from dioxin exposure," said Chartrand. "This risk is then passed on to the babies in the milk. We want our government to understand that the breast-feeding mothers of this region will not sit back and allow this incinerator to be built. It is an unacceptable risk."

The rallies were used as teach-ins where volunteers would further evangelize their neighbours. During the Adams Mine fight, the strategy of building decentralized local cells of resistance had proven very effective. This approach was now being replicated across a much broader region. Ruth and Merv Anthony organized local people in the Matheson-Cochrane region. To the south, along the length of Highway 11 and the Highway 401 communities, local teams were being organized. Their job was to press local councils to take a hard line against the movement of PCB waste along the highway.

At the height of this campaign, Jack Layton called to tell me he was running for leader of the New Democratic Party. He asked if I could organize a meeting in Timiskaming. I asked him what he knew about incinerators. Lots, he laughed. Layton was well liked in the region because of his leadership during the Adams Mine fight. It wasn't hard to draw a large crowd to a rally in Earlton where Layton was the guest speaker. He won over the crowd with his extensive knowledge of the dangers posed by incineration. But it was his talk about rebuilding a new national political narrative that genuinely won over farm families in Timiskaming. I began to wonder if this brash city councillor from Toronto could actually find a way to speak to the concerns and hopes of people across this country.

After the meeting, Jack Layton and I spoke at length about his vision for the party. The revival of the NDP was a long shot. And yet we agreed that we had won the Adams Mine fight by not being afraid of high odds. It was during this discussion that I decided to run in the next federal election as part of the Layton team.

In mid-June 2002, Public Concern Timiskaming organized a mass car rally to deliberately slow traffic on Highway 11. The police made it clear that they would not allow any attempts to shut the highway. So our strategy was to slow down traffic instead. From Kirkland Lake and New Liskeard, over three hundred cars converged on the main highway crossing at Earlton and then engaged in a choreographed cloverleaf pattern onto side roads and back onto the main highway that was designed to bring Trans-Canada traffic to a standstill without actually putting up a blockade. The event was a media success, but it scared the hell out of the organizers. There were too many variables with the high speed of traffic on the Trans-Canada to attempt such a move again. In the interest of public safety it was decided, in the future, to find other means to flex our muscle.

The resistance campaign ran on two parallel tracks: Public Concern Timiskaming organized the grassroots response, while the dairy farm-

300-car protest against Bennett incinerator. The north- and southbound convoys met on Highway 11 at the village of Earlton. June 16, 2002. PHOTO: courtesy of Kathy Hakola

ers played a leadership role within the larger Temiskaming Federation of Agriculture. Both sides worked closely together, but the farmers were adamant that they alone spoke for the agricultural sector. The farmers knew the horror stories of PCB-dioxin. That same year in Albertville, France, dioxin contamination from an incinerator forced the slaughter of five thousand cattle.[32] In 1999, a mere fifty milligrams of dioxin contamination caused losses of US$3 billion to the agriculture of Belgium. Thus even tiny amounts of contamination could be catastrophic to the $100-million-a-year industry in Timiskaming.

The farmers were nervous. In the area of food safety, perception is everything, and they were very sensitive about raising the issue of dioxin contamination in dairy products. They were equally concerned about Timiskaming being branded as the new destination for PCBs and dioxin.[33]

Thus the work with the farm community required a great deal of discussion and diplomacy.

In June 2002, however, MPP David Ramsay dramatically raised the stakes. Ramsay had initially tried to stay on the fence of the Bennett fight, but he learned again that sitting on the fence of a waste fight was like being caught in no man's land. He had to make a choice. Ramsay decided to throw in his lot against the PCB incinerator, and then set out to find a way of derailing the Bennett plan before it could go much further. Although there was no magic bullet, Ramsay thought the threat to the dairy industry could force the provincial Conservative government to bring a quick end to this deal.

On June 26, 2002, without any prior consultation with the Temiskaming Federation of Agriculture, he formally contacted milk giant Parmalat (the purchaser of all local milk) and asked the company to guarantee in writing that it would continue to purchase local dairy products if the Bennett incinerator was approved. Parmalat's response was a bombshell. They not only refused to provide this guarantee, they stated that public unease would be sufficient to terminate contracts. Senior vice president Robert Poirier was blunt. In a letter to David Ramsay he wrote: "Perception can be as damaging as reality on issues of safety. Therefore any concern from the population would force us in refusing delivery of the milk."[34]

Within a few short weeks, Dover Flour, Halton Flour Mills, and C & M Seeds publicly stated that they too would suspend purchases from Timiskaming farms if there were any questions about dioxin contamination. Ramsay had rolled the dice, and now the entire farm community was up against the wall. The farmers knew there was no sidestepping this issue. They were plunged fully into the fight. They decided to challenge Bennett's claims of safety by hiring their own experts. John Vanthof felt that local expertise had been left at a disadvantage during the Adams Mine EA because the other side hired high-priced consultants. He wasn't about to make the same mistake again.

With some members selling cows to chip in, the TFA raised $80,000 from its members (and borrowed another $40,000 from the bank—a loan that is still being paid off). They hired consultants Beak Management Consulting, with legal support from local lawyer Owen Smith.

On August 8, 2002, Vanthof and Louis Ethier released the summary report of the findings at a press conference at Queen's Park. The kicker was the line: "Beak Consulting believes the proposed incinerator poses an unacceptable risk and should not be constructed in Kirkland Lake." The TFA did not release the whole report, saying they would hold back all the data in case they needed to take the Ontario government to court.

Bennett scrambled to limit the damage of the Beak Report, hiring high-profile libel lawyer Julian Porter to demand the consultants hand it over. Porter's attack included the bizarre claim that Beak was not in a position to make accurate comment on the Bennett EA submission, because key details in the plan were being withheld from the MOE until after the project had been approved. Wrote Porter: "The EA is a planning tool and did not contain details of the storage method and protocol, transportation details and protocols, or details of the thermal process and backup systems. This will be presented in the Certification of Authorization application documents that follow the EA process."[35]

If Bennett hoped that a prestigious libel lawyer was going to scare off the farmers, he was badly mistaken. Vanthof came out swinging:

> The whole Bennett EA submission is a PR document. The company is withholding crucial information from the public and supplying us with little more than window dressing. It's outrageous that Bennett is sending its lawyers after a review team hired to ensure the basic safety of our farms. It's even more outrageous that they defend themselves with the claim that we can't critique them because they're withholding their complete plans from scrutiny.[36]

Ontario's beleaguered Ministry of Environment was looking less and less credible all the time. In a report prepared for the Canadian Environmental Law Association, Alan Levy pointed out the growing trend to allow promoters to withhold key data from public review of projects:

> The apparent trend by proponents of individual waste disposal projects (such as landfills and incinerators) is to refrain from submitting detailed design and operations plans and specifications as part of the EA. Instead the documentation is provided sometime after the EA approval has been received. The effect of this is to shield it from public scrutiny.[37]

The lines had been clearly drawn. Either Bennett was going to win or the farmers were. The region wasn't big enough for both industries.

The Ultimate Crowdsource

You couldn't blame Bennett Environmental for thinking the upcoming environmental assessment was going to be a slam dunk. Thanks to the Harris government's trashing of the EA process, rejection letters were virtually non-existent. *HighGrader Magazine* openly taunted the Ministry of Environment in a cheeky article entitled "Write Yer Own EA: The *HighGrader* Style Guide to Making Sure Your Toxic Waste Operation Is a Flying Success."[38] We pointed out that the approval rate for projects undergoing an EA in Ontario had become a staggering 98.5 per cent.

During his January 2002 visit to Northern Ontario, Dr. Paul Connett had told residents that there was no point in trusting in the Ministry of Environment to look out for their interests. "There isn't anyone protecting you but yourself. The EA in Ontario is an absolute farce."

Under the designation of the EA process for the Bennett incinerator, the only way the public could participate was through written letters of objection. But there was a kicker: the letters had to be strictly technical

Dr. Neil Carman of the Lone Star Sierra Club analyzing Bennett Environmental's EA submission with volunteer researchers Brit Griffin and Luciana Melaschenko. May 2002.

in nature. Without access to independent expertise, how was the rural population of Timiskaming to mount a credible challenge?

As we sat around the weekly war council considering whether or not to participate in such an obviously stacked process, Brenda Gold hit upon an idea. If the only option available was letters, why not drown the EA in letters? Everyone knew that the Conservatives had stripped the Ministry of Environment down to a skeleton crew. If the ministry was deluged with objections, they would be hard-pressed to process, log, and respond to them. If letters were the only tool locals had, we were going to make the most of it.

Needless to say, this was easier said than done. For starters, how was a team of amateurs to even begin writing technical letters based on the huge stack of reports? Fortunately, both Connett and Carman offered to come back up north to participate in public rallies and help train a volunteer team of researchers. Public Concern Timiskaming gathered an initial team of letter writers, including Brenda Gold, Kathy and Dennis Hakola, Brit Griffin, Anthony Story, Fran Patterson, and Luciana Melaschenko. Each of them was tasked with writing one question for every page of the report. For example, if on one page of the submission it stated that the company was using a two-inch concrete base, the letter writer could ask, what was the basis for this decision and why not a three-inch concrete base?

The initial plan was to slow the process with a flood of letters. But as the team began to read through the EA submission, numerous inconsistencies and omissions became abundantly clear. The charts and graphs were all very impressive looking, but once the team crunched the numbers, the claims didn't add up. It wasn't long before the volunteers began to itemize serious flaws in the plan. Working together, they assembled a huge array of technical objections that would be difficult for the MOE to ignore.

The team created an initial run of a thousand letters. We were determined to ensure that these letters couldn't be treated as mere form letters. Writers used different fonts. Questions were written in multiple variations. The assembled letters were then put into random groups of ten, so that one person could sign ten individual letters with ten individual objections.

A second team was then put together to write letters in French, following the same pattern. Jean-Claude Carrière from the local Franco-Ontarian organization ACFO (Association canadienne-française de l'Ontario) worked with environmental activist Lise Chartrand from the Abitibi-Témiscamingue region to organize a large francophone letter-writing campaign on both sides of the Ontario-Quebec border. At a large public meeting in New Liskeard that kicked off the campaign, the strategy was explained, and people immediately fell in love with the idea. They had been seated at long tables with paper and pens, and after they had finished signing and personalizing their own group of letters, they were given stacks of other letters in order to set up their own letter-writing clubs with neighbours.

Linda Miller and Landys Hillman went door to door getting area residents to sign letters. They took the time to put each one into an individual envelope. Other rural women held house parties where they read through the model letters and then wrote their own. Russ Mitchell, who had taken over the Public Concern Timiskaming volunteer office, took the next step of organizing letter writers into phone teams that would call the Ministry of Environment staff every day. He even provided people with a script to follow: *Have you received my letter? Have you read it? If not, why not? When will you read my letter and get back to me?*

Mitchell was originally from Chicago, where Saul Alinsky had pioneered the art of community organizing. "This is a classic Saul Alinsky tactic," he explained to me one time. "It ties up their resources, drives them crazy, and gives our people a sense that they have a way of fighting back."

On September 5, 2002, a group of PCT activists (led by Terry Graves, Lise Chartrand, Mel Booth, and myself) arrived with media in tow at the Ministry of Environment office in Toronto. We dumped sixty thousand letters—the largest letter-writing submission in MOE history—on the desk of Ariane Heisey. The ministry had to go through all the letters, catalogue them, and respond to the comments raised. They were left looking ridiculous.

During this time, Public Concern Timiskaming was given the heads-up that Fatma-Zohra Ouhachi-Vesely, the United Nations Special Rapporteur on toxic trade and human rights, was on an official visit to Canada. Grand Chief Carol McBride requested a meeting with the UN team, and local First Nation leaders met with Madame Ouhachi-Vesely in Ottawa. It was my job to prepare the technical presentation to the UN representatives, who had made it clear that they were not in Canada to get involved in any particular projects. However, Chief McBride was a top-class negotiator. On October 28, she stunned the Ministry of Environment by hosting a press conference in Toronto with Ouhachi-Vesely. The UN rapporteur publicly declared her intention to monitor the Ministry of Environment for potential human rights abuses over its failure to protect the interests of the First Nation communities during the Bennett EA process. The press conference was another PR disaster for the ministry and Bennett.

What was not known publicly was that the Ontario Ministry of Agriculture and Food (OMAF) had stepped into the fight. In a review document supplied to the Ministry of Environment, OMAF had raised serious questions about Bennett's operating record at the Saint-Ambroise incinerator. Given the potentially devastating impact of such an incinerator in the Timiskaming region, they wanted independent experts to review Bennett's record. As well, they wanted extensive baseline testing done of all agriculture and wildlife. According to OMAF, Bennett's EA submission was "based on assumptions with little supporting data."[39]

On November 1, 2002, the MOE cried uncle. They rejected the Bennett EA on the grounds that it contained a massive amount of unproven and unsubstantiated claims. In a letter to Bennett vice president Danny Ponn, the ministry laid out its objections:

> Numerous errors have been found in the EA, particularly in the air dispersion modeling [relating to human health risk assessment]. . . . There are numerous instances where the reviewer attempted to replicate the results in Tables, such as emission rates and cannot duplicate the results in the Tables using the calculations provided. . . . The examples of the deficiencies that have been found in the EA have been provided to illustrate the nature of the deficiencies; however these are just examples and not exhaustive. Bennett must go through the whole EA and Appendices to make corrections.[40]

Bennett put on a brave face and vowed to return. But it was the dead cat bounce. We had hit them so hard with the combination of organized research, resistance, and public campaigning that they were finished when they hit the canvas.

As 2002 ended, though, the hope of a quiet 2003 seemed a faint one. We already knew that the Adams Mine war would be coming back with a vengeance.

8

The Final Reel

2003–2011

It took a romantic Valentine's Day dinner in a North Bay restaurant to blow the lid off how Toronto may soon be disposing of its trash. That's when Scott Caverly, an employee of Ontario Northland Railway (ONR), happened to notice a trio of corporate lovebirds moving into a table beside him. . .

— *Now*, February 27, 2003

Walking into the Hollywood Princess off the string of strip malls along Highway 7 in Concord is like stepping into another world. The massive banquet centre is all about glamour, complete with fountains, mirrors and white columns that have served as the backdrop to countless wedding receptions and, perhaps more significantly, dozens of high-priced Tory fundraisers.
This is the world of Mario Cortellucci.

— *The Toronto Star*, May 9, 2003

Filling the Bathtub

THROUGHOUT the Bennett campaign, the Adams Mine proposal had appeared to be dormant. But the issue would never go away as long as Notre Development had a Certificate of Approval to accept waste at South Pit. Removing that Certificate of Approval was not going to be easy. Stan Gorzalczynski, who worked as a design technologist for Wabi Iron foundry in New Liskeard, believed it could be done. Since the first days of the Adams Mine project, he had pressed the hired consultants with hard-hitting questions about the unresolved problems surrounding their modelling premise. From his work at Wabi Iron, Gorzalczynski knew that there was a world of difference between a computer model and how things actually work in the real world. The more evasive the consultants were to his questions, the more convinced he was that the project was flawed.

The computer model was based on the assumption of a hole in the ground with impermeable walls. Rainwater and groundwater flowed into this hole like into a sump in a basement. According to the consultants, if you put a pump at the bottom of this sump, water and leachate could easily be contained. But the pit wasn't located at the lowest point of ground; it was more like a leaky bucket sitting on a hillside.

The computer model was little more than conjecture. Since the computer model was first proposed in 1990,[1] no one had bothered to actually measure the water levels in the pit to see how they compared to the model's predictions.

Back in late 2001, Gorzalczynski and Vanthof had jumped the fence at the Adams Mine armed with a GPS and a surveyor's transit. This was the first of a series of clandestine site visits they undertook in order to put the computer model to the test. This willingness to get in and see things for themselves stemmed from their similar backgrounds. Both men learned early how to take responsibility after they each lost their immigrant fathers to work-related accidents—Vanthof's father had died in a farming accident while Stanislaw Gorzalczynski Sr. had been killed at the Kerr-Addison Mine when Stan was nine. Stan Gorzalczynski had the technical brilliance to excel at any Ivy League engineering program, but such options were beyond reach for the son of an immigrant mining widow. Instead, showing an ability to pay attention to the details of the operation, he had quickly worked his way up through the foundry.

Arriving at South Pit, Vanthof and Gorzalczynski saw that the walls displayed the reality of the water flow in dramatic relief. For two hundred feet above the level of the surface water, the pit walls were discoloured and damp from the continual seepage through the rock face. The seepage line ran around the pit like the ring in a dirty bathtub. Above the two-hundred-foot level, the rock wall was dry as a bone—this was the line showing where the pit made contact with the water table.

The pair established transit lines, checked their GPS readings, painted lines on the rock face wall, and took photographs. The premise of hydraulic containment was based on the inflow of water with no leakage into the surrounding fractures. Thus it should be fairly straightforward to calculate the steady rise of rainwater and spring melt in the pit.

This is how Gorzalczynski explains it: "Whenever you evaluate a project proposal, you have to look at the most fundamental underpinning, and the water balance was key to the Adams Mine. If you're going to claim that a bathtub can hold water, you should be able to calculate how quickly the bathtub fills if you add two gallons per second."

But when they began measuring the level of water in the pit, it was clear that the rise of the water had levelled off. Even if they allowed for evaporation, or a season of low rainfall, the modelling predictions for how much water should have accumulated over the last ten years weren't in the ballpark. Gorzalczynski had checked the precipitation records over the last number of years and, if anything, there should have been even more water in the pit than the dump proponents' model predicted. Given the amount of water that should be flowing into the pit, it was obvious that an enormous amount of water was also leaving the pit. But where was it going?

They then headed over to nearby Round Lake. On the provincial geological maps, there was a geological dyke structure that looked like an underground pipeline from South Pit to Round Lake. As they measured the water levels at Round Lake, they found the water sat at the exact same height above sea level as the water level at South Pit. Both bodies of water were somehow connected, and the balance of water between the two lakes was as precise as the flat line you see measuring height with a water level on a construction site.

Vanthof and Gorzalczynski looked at each other stunned. "For me, this was the 'holy fuck' moment," Vanthof recalls.

As Gorzalczynski puts it, "It was clear that South Pit wasn't going to rise anymore. We had found the drain that led right into Round Lake. Ambrose Raftis had been right all along, but nobody believed him. Dr. Larry Jensen had been right. He had even calculated the outflow [of water] and nobody had listened, but standing at the pit, we were able to measure it for ourselves."

South Pit had become part of a geological flow-through lake structure connecting it to surrounding water bodies.[2] This is what the locals had been saying for years. Gorzalczynski knew it was not enough to offer their conclusion based on one reading. The water level in the pit had to be documented over the coming year to determine if spring runoff or evaporation had any effect on the overall levels. And even if they proved the pit leaked, evidence from a technologist and a farmer would not be sufficient to change the minds at the Ministry of Environment. The MOE had been consistently hostile to opponents of the dump. Senior bureaucrats had provided their own personal imprimatur on the project. As well, the new environment minister, Chris Stockwell, had publicly committed to reviving the Adams Mine deal.[3]

The pair needed a credible "expert" to validate their work. The huge stumbling block was that the hydrogeology industry in Ontario was an old boys' club and they were unlikely to find someone willing to challenge the work of the big consultant companies like Golder, Gartner Lee, and SENES who had worked for the promoter over the years.

After some research, Vanthof found the perfect choice—Ken Howard from the University of Toronto. Dr. Howard was a no-nonsense authority on underground water flows. He had no ties to industry. What's more, the Province of Ontario had chosen him as the lead hydrogeological investigator into the recent Walkerton E. coli disaster. If Howard agreed to examine their evidence, and if he agreed to take it forward, the MOE would have a very hard time challenging the man they entrusted the lives of Ontarians with during the Walkerton investigation. But these were two very large ifs.

Valentine's Day Massacre

"We hope the pit doesn't leak, but if it does, fuck it."

Perhaps it was the wine, perhaps it was a little bit of machismo, but Gordon McGuinty and his pals were less than discreet when they sat down for a St. Valentine's Day supper in 2003 at Churchill's Prime Rib House in North Bay.

Churchill's is the kind of cigar and steak joint where North Bay business owners go to put on their game face. For an entire year, McGuinty had been a pariah in both business and politics, but here he was back at Churchill's making big plans with top CN executives Keith Heller and Scott Roberts. CN was considering the purchase of the financially troubled Ontario Northland Railway. McGuinty had pitched them the added bonus of picking up a piece of the Adams Mine. He had reason to be optimistic. Republic Services' contract was running into grassroots political backlash in Michigan and maybe, if the boys played their cards right, Toronto garbage might still end up at the Adams Mine.

CN's interest came as McGuinty's finances were, once again, crumbling. Aecon's short infatuation with the project had dried up. The CIBC was after him for long-outstanding loans.[4] His attempt to sign up New York City as a client for the Adams Mine had gone nowhere. He had even tried to sell the site to his competitors at Republic. They politely told him no thanks.

Nonetheless, guardian angel Blake Wallace had lined up a whole series of new investors. The big fish in this new gang was construction magnate Mario Cortellucci, who had been the Daddy Warbucks of the Common Sense Revolution. Through his relatives and related companies in the Cortellucci-Montemarano Group, Cortellucci became the single largest donor to the party, having donated one million dollars to the Harrisites. During the leadership race to replace Harris, the Cortellucci group provided over $185,000 to leadership hopefuls Ernie Eves, Jim Flaherty, Tony Clement, and Chris Stockwell.[5]

A number of Canadian investors joined Mario Cortellucci in this new investment. They hid their identities behind numbered company 1532382 Ontario Inc., registered in suburban Don Mills, Ontario. Notre quietly transferred ownership of the site to this numbered company, which became the main player behind the newly minted Adams Mine Rail Haul Corporation. Operational control moved from McGuinty's North Bay office to Cortellucci's headquarters at the Hollywood Princess banquet hall in Concord, Ontario. Cortellucci ran high-powered political fundraisers for the Progressive Conservative Party out of the hall. He held an annual dinner that netted the party $300,000 in a single evening.[6]

And yet Notre knew that, even with these new secret partners, getting this deal off the ground would take a great deal of cunning. But cunning requires discretion, something that appeared to be missing among the three men having dinner at Churchill's restaurant that evening.

As McGuinty, Heller, and Roberts made their way to their table, they failed to notice they were sitting beside ONR union activist Scott Caverly, who was with his wife looking to celebrate a quiet St. Valentine's Day supper. The local rail unions had long been supporters of the Adams Mine plan, but Caverly was less than impressed with CN's corporate record. As soon as the men sat down, Heller, the senior vice president with CN, stated, "Let's get this strategy session underway."[7]

According to Caverly, the discussion centred on a campaign to foster public resistance in Michigan. The way Caverly remembered it, CN's role was to "actively" stop Republic's trucking efforts into Michigan while "buying off" Northern Ontario communities with the promise of economic investment.

Gordon McGuinty, for his part, was courting Southern Ontario mayors in the hope of forcing the new premier to take action against Toronto's deal with Republic. In a letter to Sarnia mayor Mike Bradley, McGuinty claimed the Adams Mine could be up and running in eighteen months.[8]

The St. Valentine's dinner mates had reason to hope that the Michigan contract could be derailed. By early 2003, the Don't Trash Michigan campaign had grown into a coalition of twenty-one environmental, religious, and civic groups. They wanted action from U.S. federal and state representatives to push back against the growing landfill industry in the state.

Michigan was importing 3.6 million tonnes of waste annually from nearby states. On top of that, another 1.78 million tonnes were coming from the GTA. Three Michigan politicians—John Dingell, Debbie Stabenow, and Mike Rogers—played leading roles in trying to stop the Republic contract. All three introduced bills calling for an end to Canadian garbage imports, and all three had received campaign contributions from CN.[9]

As the dinner went on and the strategy talk expanded, Caverly heard one of the men make the statement, "We hope the pit doesn't leak, but if it does, f–k it."[10]

Caverly left the restaurant and briefed his union local about what had been said at the meeting. ONR union president Brian Stevens held a press conference to challenge CN.[11] Both McGuinty and Scott Roberts attended. Stevens held nothing back. He repeated the comment about the pit leaking. This wasn't good press for CN. Roberts told the media these comments had either been misunderstood or they were malicious in nature. But when Stevens saw McGuinty and Roberts standing at the back of the press conference, he shouted at them, "It's a small town. Next time, don't eat at Churchill's."

Whatever CN's interest in the project may have been, they quickly went to ground and were careful not to be seen anywhere near the Adams Mine project again.

The Secret Land Deal

The request seemed simple enough. "I would like to see the file on the sale of two thousand acres of Crown land adjacent to the Adams Mine."

Responding to questions about the sale of public lands is a regular part of the work of the Ministry of Natural Resources (MNR). Crown land sales are posted online at the Environmental Bill of Rights Registry. Large or controversial land sales involve consultation and a public comment period, but the front-line staffer at the Kirkland Lake district office was evasive. "What sale are you talking about?"

"I would like to see the file on the sale of two thousand acres of former mining claims adjacent to the Adams Mine," I replied. "I would like to see the agreement for the lands in question, as well as the appraisal that pegged this sale at twenty-two dollars an acre."

I was with MPP Gilles Bisson and local provincial NDP candidate Ben Lefebvre. To help jog the MNR's memory, I itemized every document that was in the MNR folder pertaining to this particular land sale.[12] We were quickly ushered into a side room. MNR officials buzzed about nervously.

Finally, a senior staffer came into the room. "We don't know what you're talking about," he said.

"Are you telling me that the sale of two thousand acres of public land is being done in secret?"

It was the afternoon of April 4, 2003, and the normally sedate office of Ministry of Natural Resources in Kirkland Lake was on the verge of a political shitstorm. For months, the sale of two thousand acres of Crown land had been quietly negotiated between MNR staff and Gordon McGuinty on behalf of 1532382 Ontario Inc. Both sides agreed on a fire-sale deal of twenty-two dollars an acre. Within the MNR, staff had raised objections that the price was outrageously low—staff pegged the land value at between forty-eight and seventy-eight dollars an acre, which meant 1532382 Ontario Inc.'s price was less than half the low end[13]—but these concerns had been smoothed over. To facilitate the sale, the MNR hand-delivered the offer of sale to McGuinty's office in North Bay in February 2003. It was all going through very hush-hush and strictly on the q.t. That is, until a source called us with a detailed heads-up on the projected sale.

The land in question comprised old tailings dams that held the waste residue of the Adams Mine iron ore operations. The purchase of this land had been stipulated by the 1998 EA hearing as essential for ensuring adequate wetlands for the annual discharge of hundreds of millions of litres of contaminated water. The only problem was that Notre hadn't gotten around to fulfilling this condition. They had held off purchasing the land after the EA approval came through, and took no steps to purchase it as the 2000 vote was being undertaken. Now, in 2003, without a contract in sight, they seemed to need this land very badly. If Gordon McGuinty's new partners were going to have a chance at selling the dump, they needed to make it look like a dump. The only way to do that was to pump out the clear water that had become the focus of so much attention.

Our appearance at the MNR office, however, suddenly put the land deal in doubt. Their refusal to confirm or deny the sale was little more than a stopgap. By Monday morning the storm clouds were beginning to form. New Liskeard lawyer Owen Smith (acting on my behalf) sent a letter to MNR coordinator Vic Prasad calling for an immediate suspension of the sale.[14] This request was followed by letters from the Algonquin Tribal Council and Wabun Tribal Council demanding consultations before any sale was allowed to proceed.

MNR district manager Craig Greenwood attempted to push back by responding that the issue of the land transfer had been addressed as part of the provincial EA. "The matter of Crown land acquisitions was identified in the proponent's environmental assessment and is not subject to any further considerations under the Environmental Assessment Act."[15]

But this wasn't the case at all. The Adams Mine EA had specifically scoped out key issues such as the pumping of water onto the adjacent tailing lands. As well, Timiskaming First Nation, which had identified its long-standing historic interest in the territory, had been left out of the EA process by both the Ministry of Environment and the Ministry of Natural Resources.

The MNR knew this was a major problem. Greenwood had privately warned senior MNR staff that there could be problems with the sale of the land because of a lack of consultations with Timiskaming First Nation. Prior to the finalization of the sale, the MNR sent a letter to Notre advising them that the land deal could be affected by a land claim from Timiskaming First Nation.[16] But the MNR hadn't given a heads-up to the First Nations. If all had gone according to plan, this sweetheart deal would have been concluded without any First Nation community knowing that the sale was under way.

Now that the news of the sale was public, the MNR scrambled to contain the damage. When we were able to link Mario Cortellucci to this backroom sale of Crown land, the story turned into a political firestorm. We had known for some months about the Cortellucci agreement to purchase the Adams Mine and had been trying to expose the investors in the numbered company when we learned about the sale of Crown land to 1532382 Ontario Inc. Outing Cortellucci's role drew front-page headlines in the major dailies. Everything about the land sale reeked of insider influence. The Eves government was now facing a full-blown scandal.

"Why were you planning to sell Crown land to the largest donators of the PC Party without any public notice and at below market prices?" MPP Ramsay challenged Deputy Premier Elizabeth Witmer (who had received $40,000 in donations from Cortellucci) in the Ontario Legislature on May 7, 2003. "If you sell them the land, they stand to make hundreds of millions of dollars. Minister, do you really expect us to believe that it is just coincidence that the largest donor to the Ontario PC party was involved in a secret deal to buy Crown Land at $22 an acre?"[17]

As the news of the land scandal broke, we found out that Canadian Waste Services had launched a lawsuit contesting Cortellucci's ownership of the Adams Mine property. CWS had a $4.6 million lien on the property and claimed a right of first refusal over any other deals connected to the mine site.[18]

A fight between the Cortelluccis and Canadian Waste Services was a golden opportunity to shine a light on the Cortellucci agreement. We also began to receive brown manila envelopes from Cortellucci's political enemies and competitors. By early June, a new scandal erupted when it was revealed that the Cortellucci group of companies had received $36.3 million in loans from the Ontario Pension Board to help purchase seven rural properties in Brampton and Vaughan. No other construction companies had been offered similar loans. What's worse, Pension Board chair Don Weiss had been the executive fundraiser for the Progressive Conservative Party from 1992 to 2000.[19] Given Cortellucci's largesse in terms of political donations, this was another deal that stank of backroom favours.

As Queen's Park opposition hammered the government over this secret sale of public land, Public Concern Timiskaming galvanized our grassroots volunteers. Public meetings and rallies were held. Letter-writing campaigns were initiated. We then hit upon the idea of putting in a counterbid with two thousand people pledging to purchase one acre each at the price of thirty dollars an acre. With a higher bid on the table, why was the MNR pushing through with an underpriced sale of Crown land?

Notre knew the deal was in trouble. On April 10, 1532382 Ontario Inc. sent a cheque for $51,360 to the MNR demanding they complete the sale of land. The cheque was placed in a safe at the office of the MNR and wasn't touched. By April 17, senior MNR staff decided to stop the land sale altogether until there was some clear direction from the government.[20]

The Cortellucci team was rattled. According to one of our sources, the investors requested that "Mike" be brought in for a special meeting at the Hollywood Princess in order to help put the land deal back on track. It didn't take much sleuthing to figure out who Mike was. Nonetheless, we knew we'd need to document the connection.

When the mysterious members of 1532382 Ontario Inc. showed up for a meeting at the Hollywood Princess on May 14, 2003, they didn't notice the private eye in the parking lot with a camera. He was documenting everyone entering and leaving, as well as getting lists of their licence plates. The detective provided Public Concern Timiskaming with a clear picture of the investors and players in the numbered company. But the prize of the day was the photograph the gumshoe took of Mike Harris and Mario Cortellucci outside the Hollywood Princess.

We don't know what Harris discussed during this meeting, but as they say, a picture is worth a thousand words. I passed the photograph to MPP Gilles Bisson, who walked into Queen's Park question period and held up the photograph. "Is Mr. Harris now an investor in that project? I'd like to know. Is he? Is that why they were meeting? Is he trying to help out in the sale of the land, or the expedition of the sale of the land?"[21]

Richard Brennan of *The Toronto Star* called me to find out why we had hired a private investigator to track Mike Harris's involvement in the meeting. "Do you think it's appropriate to spy on the activities of a private citizen?" he asked.

"We're not spying on private citizens," I replied. "We're keeping tabs on Mike Harris and his ongoing involvement in the Adams Mine. We make no apologies for exposing his backroom shenanigans."

Showdown with the Ministry

Ken Howard wasn't an activist, he was an academic. He had little interest in being drawn into a political battle, but he did agree to look at the evidence supplied by John Vanthof and Stan Gorzalczynski. As Dr. Howard reviewed their findings, he realized there were major problems with the 1998 EA decision. Early in the spring of 2003, Vanthof approached Environment Minister Chris Stockwell with the same information, but Stockwell wasn't interested. The erratic Harris loyalist was an outspoken advocate of the Adams Mine. During his ill-fated run to replace Mike Harris, Stockwell had vowed to make the project a reality come hell or high water.[22]

Stockwell's big problem was that he didn't know when to keep his mouth shut and his head down. As the Eves government struggled to distance itself from the growing Cortellucci scandal, Stockwell decided it was time to raise the Adams Mine banner. On May 26, 2003, he called a meeting with officials from Toronto, York, and Peel where he told them, like it or not, the Adams Mine was coming. They had eighteen months to get their act together. The meeting was behind closed doors, but within hours of the meeting, sources at City Hall had given Terry Graves a very clear picture of Stockwell's attempt to push the Adams Mine back. Naturally, the Adams Mine Coalition challenged Stockwell immediately.

But the bully days of Mike Harris were over. Eves was in trouble, and Stockwell didn't have the backup he needed to pick a garbage fight with Canada's biggest city. On the same day as Stockwell waded into the Toronto garbage fight, the Timiskaming farmers held a press conference at Queen's Park with Ken Howard. They accused Stockwell and Premier

Eves of ignoring evidence that the Adams Mine EA decision was flawed.

"It was irresponsible for Minister Stockwell to reject, out of hand, evidence about the safety of this site," stated John Vanthof. "This is our ministry. He is our minister. It is the minister's job to ensure this site is safe. It shouldn't have to fall to farmers to hire experts to prove that our groundwater will be safe."

But it was the presence of Dr. Howard at the press conference that drew the attention. "I've seen enough red flags to make me very concerned that decisions have been made that are incorrect," said Howard about the Adams Mine EA. "In fact, those flags seem to have been ignored."[23]

Howard's involvement posed a major problem for both the Conservative government and the MOE. His credentials on the E. coli investigation at Walkerton were impeccable. Other than Ipperwash, no other incident was as politically toxic to the Common Sense Revolution as the water tragedy at Walkerton. When Howard spoke, people listened.

Stockwell was in too much political trouble to have the credibility to take on Howard. He had received money from Cortellucci during his run for party leader. Within a day of the press conference, opposition members in the legislature then exposed the fact that his brother was involved in the deal to revive the Adams Mine project.[24] Stockwell's attempt to promote the Adams Mine while ignoring the evidence of the farmers smelled of the old-boy politics that were dragging down the Eves government. More political dirt was soon dug up, and within two weeks, he was forced to resign in disgrace from a spending scandal over his expenses.[25]

Stockwell's political flameout only added to the problems faced by the new Adams Mine promoters. Knowing that their much-coveted Certificate of Approval was on the line, they came out swinging. For four straight weeks, Adams Mine Rail Haul paid for full-page ads in *The Temiskaming Speaker* calling John Vanthof a liar and making the claim that the "ADAMS MINE DOES NOT LEAK."

This media attack may have been an attempt to discredit Vanthof, but it was also aimed at pushing the Ministry of Natural Resources to ratify the land deal. In an e-mail to MNR senior staffer John Burke, McGuinty referenced the attack ads and urged the ministry not to engage in any consultation with the "Natives."

> I understand there may be a decision to consult with the Natives prior to closing the agreed land transaction. I strongly suggest the government and the MNR do not make this move. . . . I suggest you and your staff look at this week's Temiskaming Speaker wherein our ad addresses the lies of the TFA. . . . if the government proceeds with a consultation with the natives they will look ridiculous.[26]

Notre partner Gord Acton then sent the MNR a threat of legal action for $50 million demanding the land be immediately turned over. Adams Mine Rail Haul followed up with a $10 million lawsuit against both John Vanthof and the Temiskaming Federation of Agriculture. Their claim was based on the premise that, since the farmers had not given their evidence to the proponent prior to going public, they had damaged the business potential for Adams Mine Rail Haul.

The Adams Mine backers clearly couldn't sue Ken Howard. The optics would have been atrocious. However, if they thought they could spook off either Vanthof or Howard, they were mistaken. Within a day of the lawsuit being issued, Howard released a damning summary of his analysis of the Adams Mine modelling.

Howard pointed out that the Certificate of Approval had been issued despite the fact that the evidence of the two later drill holes (DH-98-1 and DH-98-2) contradicted the predictions of the model. As Howard stated in his report, "The data from the two boreholes must have sent 'shock-waves' through the proponent's camp." The low water pressure threw the whole premise into doubt. Nonetheless, the director of the Ministry of Environment had allowed Golder to make up a new model to incorporate these low results, a model that Howard described as "virtually worthless" and having "no scientific merit."

In his report, Howard made it clear he didn't blame Golder. The consultants were simply attempting to find a way to "present [their] client's data in the best possible light." Howard wasn't nearly as understanding when it came to the role of the MOE. According to Howard, it was the role of the director of the ministry to protect the public interest, and the MOE failed in this role. "The Director had no qualms about making a decision based on the findings of two seriously flawed models that should have been rejected without hesitation."[27]

Senior Ministry of Environment engineer David Staseff, who had testified in support of the proposal at the EA Board, had the task of rebutting Howard. "It is probable that Dr. Howard does not fully understand the design and operations for this proposed landfill," he stated in an internal memo.[28] He also accused Howard of not having actually visited the site. "This is unacceptable," he stated. It was also untrue.

Howard had visited the site. He just hadn't bothered to inform the MOE. Staseff's objections were ironic given that, just prior to the approval of the project in 1998, he was the recipient of an internal memo that warned that the premise was "based on several assumptions which cannot be verified in the field."[29]

The Temiskaming Federation of Agriculture refused to hand over the full Howard report to the ministry, stating they would reserve it for a court action being commenced against the Ministry of Environment. But the three-page summary was damning enough. Nonetheless, the MOE tried to shrug off Howard's accusations. Rob Campbell of the ministry told *HighGrader Magazine*: "It may seem like strong language to those who don't understand science but in reality it is really pretty weakly worded and doesn't tell us anything. It is just one professor at one university saying this."[30]

Howard, however, was not about to back off. "The level of scientific ignorance demonstrated by the Ontario Ministry of Environment with regards to the Adams Mine, never ceases to amaze me. . . . [they are ignoring] the potentially catastrophic loss of hydraulic containment at the site."[31]

The $10 million lawsuit against the farmers put the Ministry of Environment in an even worse light. The premise of the suit was that if citizens were forced to take it upon themselves to do the work of the MOE, then they could be held liable for interfering with the business interests of a project's proponents. Matters were coming to a head. But nothing would be decided until after another provincial election, set for October 2, 2003.

McGuinty versus McGuinty

The electoral victory of Dalton McGuinty's Liberals was widely seen as the final nail in the Adams Mine coffin. Throughout the years in opposition, Dalton McGuinty had managed to avoid getting involved in the Adams Mine controversy, and MPP David Ramsay often seemed alone in the Liberal caucus on the issue. Nonetheless, the final rejection of the Adams Mine dump seemed assured by the resounding defeat of the Progressive Conservative government.

Ramsay was appointed minister of natural resources. MNR staff began outreach with area First Nations regarding the outstanding land consultations over the proposed sale of two thousand acres. The big problem for the provincial MNR was recognizing the land interests of Timiskaming First Nation. Negotiations with a Quebec-based Band that had never surrendered land rights in Ontario would be precedent setting. Nonetheless, Chris Maher, deputy director of the Land Claims Negotiations Branch, began making outreach to TFN to deal with their land concerns.

Ministry staff established formal consultations with Timiskaming, Beaverhouse, Matachewan, and Temagami First Nations. I had the responsibility for setting up the negotiations on behalf of TFN and the Algonquin Nation Secretariat. I worked closely with MNR staffers on the framework for negotiations on the issues relating to Aboriginal title of the property. One of the MNR officials later confided that as soon as they began the consultations with Timiskaming First Nation they knew the writing was on the wall. "We were fucked as soon as we saw the documentation you guys had."

But even as this process began moving forward, the Ministry of Environment once again played the spoiler. On November 14, 2003, the MOE stunned everyone by approving a permit by Adams Mine Rail Haul to drain all water from South Pit, giving the public thirty days to comment. An editorial in the *Sault Star* asked why the pit was being drained if there were no plans on the government's part to push the project back onto centre stage.

> Ontario Premier Dalton McGuinty insists there are no plans to convert the abandoned Adams Mine into a dump. If that's the case, we wonder why a permit has been issued to allow the mine owners to pump millions of litres of water a day from the pit. Clearly, the Cortelluccis aren't going to use that water to irrigate the surrounding farm fields.[32]

This move ignited a firestorm in the north. How was it possible that a government ministry would issue a permit to pump 26 million litres of water a day onto land that was the subject of ongoing First Nation consultations? What was the rush to drain the pit, with no possible waste contract on the horizon? Even more ominous—why would the ministry allow the pit to be drained while it was locked in a public dispute with Ken Howard about the water levels in the pit? Public Concern Timiskaming immediately accused the MOE of attempting to destroy important evidence.

Within weeks, 24,000 letters of opposition had deluged the Ministry of Environment office. Timiskaming First Nation warned of another round of blockades to prevent pumps from being installed at the site. "Emotions are running very high in this district," said Terry Graves. "Certainly I expect that if the government doesn't do the right thing, actions will be taken."[33]

Charlie Angus leading a workshop on writing letters to oppose the Adams Mine Rail Haul bid to dewater South Pit. Riverside Place, New Liskeard, 2003.

The new environment minister, Leona Dombrowsky, appeared to be caught like a deer in the headlights. Graves attempted to reach out to the minister: "This is a young government with lots of goodwill in its court," he said. "But unfortunately, a very tense situation is brewing. I am asking Ms. Dombrowksy to sit down with us and find a way of defusing this potentially explosive situation."[34]

The new Liberal government now found itself embroiled in the same politics that had burned so many other politicians. In Timiskaming, David Ramsay went from hero to zero overnight. His phone was ringing off the hook. Dalton McGuinty was Gordon's distant cousin. Public Concern Timiskaming ran an advertisement showing both men under the ad line "Kissing Cousins: Is Blood Thicker Than Groundwater?"

Ramsay clearly didn't have a picture of what was going on in his own government. Had a Ministry of Environment staffer gone rogue? Was Ramsay's cabinet doing an end run on his constituents? When pushed by media, Ramsay vowed that he would quit the government if the Adams Mine went ahead.

Notre attempted to exert counterpressure. They launched a $301 million lawsuit against the provincial government demanding the immediate turnover of the two thousand acres being negotiated with the First Nations. For their part, the Temiskaming Federation of Agriculture threatened to launch a lawsuit against Environment Minister Dombrowsky. "We refuse to be just another broken election promise," declared dairy farmer Louis Ethier at a press conference in Toronto.

The new Liberal government was learning what its predecessors had learned to their detriment, that the Adams Mine was politically radioactive. Following a tense meeting in Toronto with farm leaders and First Nation leaders, Dombrowsky agreed to set up a high-level meeting with MOE staff and Ken Howard.

On December 2, 2003, Dr. Howard supplied his full report to the MOE. The ministry accepted Howard's conclusion about the fundamental flaws in the model.[35] MOE staff then drew up a plan for following through on Howard's recommendations for further study of the site. After years of controversy, the ministry recognized that the original two-dimensional model was fundamentally flawed.

The MOE study never took place. On April 5, 2004, the Liberal government decided instead to kill the Adams Mine project once and for all. They introduced the Adams Mine Lake Act, which made it illegal in the Province of Ontario to dump garbage in any site that was, or had taken on, the attributes of a lake. The original Adams Mine investors were paid out for expenses.

The investors who had joined 1532382 Ontario Inc. refused to accept the payout. They tried to push ahead with a $300 million lawsuit against the Province of Ontario, which provincial courts quickly bounced out the door.

This time, we thought, it was really over.

The Mysterious Vito Gallo

The Adams Mine Lake Act was passed in April 2004. That June, I ran for the New Democrats and won the federal riding of Timmins–James Bay by just over six hundred votes (I would be re-elected on a much more solid footing eighteen months later). Mayor Bill Enouy of Kirkland Lake was the first local politician to call me and express a desire to work together. We had been on opposite sides of the Adams Mine battle for years, but his willingness to reach out spoke of the desire of local people to finally turn the page.

The war over Adams Mine would have one last gasp. On October 30, 2006, an obscure American citizen named Vito Gallo launched a $355 million lawsuit against the Canadian government. He claimed to be the sole owner of the Adams Mine property and sued Canada under the Chapter 11 provisions of NAFTA over the loss of investments that were due him as an American citizen. No one associated with this seventeen-year debacle had heard of Gallo before.

A NAFTA challenge was only open to American investors who had been expropriated under Canadian law. The problem was that 1532382 Ontario Inc. had been constructed as a deal with ten key Canadian investors.[36] Gallo didn't appear to have put any money into the deal.

According to Gallo's statement of claim, the Canadian investors had transferred their investment to a single share that was given to him. He provided no evidence of his involvement in the project. During its short life, the numbered company had secured no waste contracts and made no investments at the site. Nonetheless, Gallo's lawyers were asking an international trade tribunal to award him millions in compensation from Canadian taxpayers.

In the House of Commons, I hammered Trade Minister David Emerson about the issue. I pointed out the financial connections between senior federal Conservative cabinet ministers (Jim Flaherty, Stockwell Day, and Tony Clement) and the Cortellucci group.

An American investor named Vito Gallo is going after the Canadian taxpayer for $350 million in compensation over the failed Adams Mine dump proposal. . . . Mr. Speaker, I would like to offer some guidance. I researched the Adams Mine land titles and I could not find the name Gallo because of course it is a numbered company. I did, however, find the name Mario Cortellucci, who is a very close friend of the Conservative Party. The Cortellucci clan has given $170,000 recently, including $50,000 to our present finance minister when he was running for provincial leadership, $10,000 to the health minister when he was running, and $60,000 to that party's coffers since 2004. Would the minister phone up super Mario and ask him to help the government find out just who is going to stand to benefit from this massive hit on Canadian taxpayers?[37]

After question period, Emerson came over to me. He seemed genuinely perplexed by the Gallo challenge and asked me what I knew about the case. I told him I had an office full of documents on the Cortellucci involvement in the Adams Mine property. It isn't common for a minister to ask a member of the opposition to share evidence on a politically sensitive file, but Emerson requested that I meet with his officials. I turned over documents relating to the corporate structure and involvement of the Cortellucci Group of Companies in 1532382 Ontario Inc.

Although the Justice Department lawyers took the position that Gallo's claim was ridiculous, they nonetheless took the tribunal hearing very seriously. In preparation, they relied on the expertise of some of the key people who had spent years fighting this project. Canada's argument was that shutting down the Adams Mine project was "a bona fide measure taken for the public good" in consideration of "protecting and ensuring safe drinking water." And further, that "the Adams Mine could threaten the safety of local water resources in Timiskaming." For the people who had fought this dubious project for almost two decades, it was sweet recognition to know that the basis of their opposition had become Canada's official position.

The mysterious Mr. Gallo wanted the entire hearing kept from the public. While some issues were redacted, the veil was turned back on this mysterious investor. Turns out that at the time that 1532382 Ontario Inc. was being incorporated, he was a thirty-three-year-old government employee in Pennsylvania with no history in the waste business. His only apparent connection to the deal was that he was a cousin of Cortellucci's partner, Saverio Montemarano.

The tribunal marvelled that Gallo was unable to produce a single piece of paper to establish his claim that he was the owner of the mine site prior to the passage of the Adams Mine Lake Act. "It is inconceivable that the Claimant has not been able to produce one shred of documentary evidence confirming the date when Mr. Gallo acquired ownership: no agreement, no contract, no confirmation slip, no instruction letter, no invoice, no email—absolutely nothing."[38] Further, the tribunal determined that the shareholder minute books that purported to show Gallo signing off on documents in 2002 had actually been signed in 2008 and then backdated.

This was serious business. Gallo had taken the Government of Canada to an international trade tribunal. Never mind that he had dropped his request to $105 million in compensation, the tribunal threw out the case. Gallo was also whacked with $450,000 in costs awarded to the Government of Canada. His own legal fees could have been enormous.

So there you have it—the last attempt to squeeze a buck out of the Adams Mine ended in a humiliating spanking before a NAFTA tribunal. The South Pit of the Adams Mine will never be used as a garbage dump. It has become home to a thriving Arctic char fish farm. The fish seem to do very well in the beautifully clean waters of the pit.

Word on the street, however, has it that the investors of 1532382 Ontario Inc. are still convinced they are sitting on an ideal business opportunity. As the saying goes, some people are just too dumb to quit.

Stepping out of the Box

W HAT ARE THE LESSONS to be learned from the Adams Mine? If nothing else, it changed the way we think about waste and environmental responsibility. In the 1990s, the proposal to use a thousand years' worth of groundwater to wash twenty years' worth of garbage was presented as perfectly reasonable. Today, it would strike most Canadians as a profligate misuse of resources.

The Adams Mine was a watershed in Canadian waste management. It spelled an end to the days when urban waste strategies were based on finding a hole in the hinterlands. The Adams Mine forced politicians to get serious about recycling and waste diversion efforts, in urban centres as well as small towns and rural regions.

Politicians and industry misjudged the public's willingness to make lifestyle changes to protect the environment. Urban residents were way out in front of the politicians when it came to supporting waste diversion and curbside separation of waste. Such lessons should be kept in mind when dealing with the dismal political foot-dragging on climate change legislation.

But what are the lessons to be learned from the campaign itself?

The Adams Mine war was fought between two seemingly ill-matched sides. An isolated rural region with few economic or political resources defeated a mega-project. Such victories don't come along every day.

Industry always learns lessons from fights like the Adams Mine—in fact, failed dump promoter Gordon McGuinty now offers workshops in how promoters of contentious projects can manage dissent and media. Citizens need to do the same.

If you read McGuinty's self-published memoir, you will see that he invokes the spectre of terrorism to explain why this project went down to defeat. He goes so far as to compare the actions of local opponents to mass killer Nidal Hasan (who killed thirteen soldiers at Fort Hood). McGuinty writes: "Let's put aside the kid-gloves. . . . I am going to call it [organized opposition to the Adams Mine] for what it was: a sophisticated form of 'political terrorism.'"[1] Thus, the average people who opposed the project belong on the same continuum as a mass murderer, because they stood in the way of a billion-dollar payday.

One could write off such melodrama as the grumblings of a sore loser. But the over-the-top language reveals how much the corporate agenda can be threatened by the idea of an empowered citizenry. This is why the vilification of citizens as "extremist" or "terrorist" is an increasingly common tactic of the right wing. The Harper government routinely denounces opponents as "radical extremists." It's about putting people in boxes—making them think twice before they exercise their right to participate in public debate.

But intimidating the public is only one part of the strategy. The Adams Mine would not have made any headway if it were not for the political undermining of independent public process. The same tactics are being played out today on a much larger scale by the Harper government. Today's Conservative ministers are "contemporizing" the federal environmental assessment in the same way their Common Sense predecessors "scoped" the Adams Mine regulatory process. At the heart of this Orwellian language is a cynical gutting of objective standards for accountability.

In watching the Harperites, I see a group of narrow-minded ideologues who only listen to their own kind. That was the fundamental mistake of the Adams Mine promoters. They relied on a small echo chamber of like-minded investors, Tory insiders, and hired consultants. This narrow gene pool ran out of ideas long before the deal finally died.

Our side, however, always knew exactly whom we were fighting. Around our planning table were farmers, housewives, and First Nation people. There was no professional media team to coax us. As a team of lay people, we knew how to speak in the voice of everyday Canadians and were able to strike a chord in both the rural north and the urban south. The diversity of views within our coalition made us undefeatable. We adapted while the other side didn't.

But tactics alone did not win a fight as grinding as the Adams Mine war. We won because we were right. We won because we stayed together. This commitment to building real community is the difference between ordinary people and extremists, the difference between civic action and those who would jerry-rig the system to favour the few.

Men like Stephen Harper and Mike Harris believe that people can be diverted from the bigger issues by the politics of fear and resentment. Undermining the public process may seem like a quick road to a desired outcome, but don't underestimate the determination of Canadians to protect their democratic institutions. Canadians are reasonable and they are patient, but they aren't pushovers. If you push them, they will push back hard.

Those who put themselves on the line during the Adams Mine war taught me that politics is not about playing the game; politics is a damned serious business with enormous consequences for those who are not on the inside. We all have a stake in ensuring that legitimate public process is protected. There is a fundamental obligation to ensure that the interests of the powerful are not given free rein.

For me the most important lesson of the Adams Mine was that ordinary people have the capacity to accomplish extraordinary things for the common good. This realization is why I remain so optimistic about the future. I think of a letter the late Sandra Mitchell wrote to people in Timiskaming in December 1995 as she watched the Adams Mine being beaten for the second time: "You can be proud of the people of Timiskaming. Never underestimate the power of a people backed into a corner on their home ground."

Yes, Sandra, I am very proud of these people. It has been my great honour to learn from their wisdom and to fight like hell in the House of Commons to represent their dream of a decent life in the great country that is Canada.

Notes

INTRODUCTION: THE WATERSHED

1 Gordon McGuinty, *Trashed: How Political Garbage Made the United States Canada's Largest Dump* (Canmore: Elevation Press, 2010), pp. 143, 45.

CHAPTER 1. THE SET-UP, 1989–1991

1 P.N. Calder, "Geotechnical Review Adams Mines 1987," report for Cliffs of Canada, December 1987.

2 Dr. Larry Jensen to Mississauga City Councillor Frank Dale, e-mail, October 16, 2000.

3 Dr. Larry Jensen to Mayor Mel Lastman, letter, August 2, 2000.

4 Carrie Buchanan, "Garbage Blues," *Canadian Geographic*, February 1988.

5 McGuinty, *Trashed*.

6 Ibid., p. 9.

7 Heather Rogers, *Gone Tomorrow: The Hidden Life of Garbage* (New York: The New Press, 2005), p. 18.

8 "Metro Trucks Move Mountains of Trash," *The Toronto Star*, February 18, 1990.

9 Harold Crooks, *Giants of Garbage* (Toronto: James Lorimer and Company, 1993), p. 198.

10 Ibid., p. 213.

11 Rogers, *Gone Tomorrow*, p. 200.

12 Rhonda Hustler to Kathy Martin, letter, October 24, 1990.

13 McGuinty, *Trashed*, pp. 20–21.

14 Natural Resources Minister Lyn McLeod to Ray Black, President, Marmora TNT Committee, letter, February 28, 1990.

15 McGuinty, *Trashed*, p. 33.

16 Ibid., p. 19.

17 "Recycling Complex Disposal Proposed for Adams Mine," *Northern Daily News*, November 29, 1989.

18 McGuinty, *Trashed*, p. 74.

19 "Forthright Proposal Deserves Respect," *Northern Daily News*, December 1, 1989.

20 "Garbage by Any Other Name Spells 'Opportunity,'" *Northern Daily News*, November 23, 1989.

21 Ibid.

22 "Mine Walls Key," *Northern Daily News*, October 11, 1990.

23 McGuinty, *Trashed*, p. 41.

24 "Residents Voice Concern," *Northern Daily News*, December 6, 1989.

25 "Doctor Disputes Allegations," *Northern Daily News*, December 3, 1990.

26 "Council Stands Firm on Garbage Issue," *Northern Daily News*, August 8, 1990.

27 "Not Massaging Ego Sue Gamble Says," *Northern Daily News*, December 19, 1990.

28 "VOME Supports Adams Mine," *Northern Daily News*, December 14, 1989.

29 "Dump Vote Sought: Metro Told to Conduct Referendum," *Northern Daily News*, April 27, 1995.

30 "Gates Shut at Adams, Sherman," *Northern Daily News*, March 31, 1990.

31 "Petition for Yes," editorial, *Northern Daily News*, August 21, 1990.

32 "Notre Hosts Meeting," *Northern Daily News*, January 12, 1991.

33 "Burying Taxpayers under Pile of NDP Garbage," *The Toronto Star*, April 5, 1991 [cited in Crooks, *Giants of Garbage*].

34 "Metro Faces 'Garbage Apocalypse' Council Says," *The Toronto Star*, April 11, 1991 [cited in Crooks, *Giants of Garbage*].

35 "An Abandoned Northern Mine Might Yet Be Destination for Toronto's Garbage," *Maclean's*, February 26, 2001.

CHAPTER 2. INVASION OF THE PROCESS SNATCHERS, 1995

1 Brit Griffin, "Waking the Sleeping Giant," *HighGrader Magazine*, Summer 1995.

2 Brit Griffin, "A Community Response to the Adams Mine Landfill Proposal," REEPA, 1996.

3 Environmental Assessment Board of Ontario, EAB Decision: Notre Development Corporation, June 19, 1996, p. 17.

4 "Adams Dump Protestors Raise Stink as Harris Visits Earlton," *Northern Daily News*, June 8, 1995.

5 "Harris Dumps Waste Agency: KL Mine Looks Good," *The Toronto Star*, July 6, 1995.

6 "Two Options for Garbage Disposal," *The Toronto Star*, July 7, 1995.

7 "Communities Welcome News That Mega Dumps Cancelled," *The Toronto Star*, July 6, 1995.

8 Ibid.

9 "Ontario Government Axes Interim Waste Authority," *The Temiskaming Speaker*, July 12, 1995.

10 "Raftis' Arrest Sparks Flames at Garbage Meeting," *The Temiskaming Speaker*, June 14, 1995.

11 Minutes of Public Liaison Committee #1, Bon Air Motor Inn, Kirkland Lake, June 12, 1995.

12 Ibid.

13 "Metro Solution under Discussion," *Northern Daily News*, April 25, 1995.

14 Minutes of PLC #1, June 12, 1995.

15 Minutes of Public Liaison Committee Meeting, Legion Hall, Kirkland Lake, October 30, 1995.

16 "Notre Slams Farmers," *Northern Daily News*, July 15, 1995.

17 Robert Power to Gary Struthers, letter, July 14, 1995.

18 Gary Struthers to Robert Power, letter, July 14, 1995.

19 Stan Gorzalczynski, letter to the editor, *The Temiskaming Speaker*, July 14, 1995.

20 "'Biggest Fraud' MPP Demands Mayor Keep Election Promise," *Northern Daily News*, August 11, 1995.

21 "Adams Mine Fight Hits Court," *Northern Daily News*, September 11, 1995.

22 "Ramsay Refuses to Apologize," *The Temiskaming Speaker*, September 13, 1995.

23 "The Numbers Speak Out," *Northern Daily News*, September 1, 1995.

24 Tracy Boulay, "Residents Not Being Listened To," letter to the editor, *Northern Daily News*, October 7, 1995.

25 Doris Morrison, "Reeve Was Right On!" *Northern Daily News*, October 12, 1995.

26 Boulay, "Residents Not Being Listened To."

27 Golder Associates Ltd. (K.G. Lesarge and D.R. Brown), "Preliminary Hydrogeo-logical Investigation, Adams Mine, Kirkland Lake, Ontario," report to M.M. Dillon Limited, December 1990, 51 pages + attachments.

28 Golder, "Preliminary Hydrogeological Review and Landfill Development Feasibil-ity," June 1990, p. 23.

29 "Lake Temiskaming Threatened by Metro Proposal Says Consultant," *The Temiska-ming Speaker*, December 13, 1995.

30 EAB Decision: Notre Development Corporation, June 19, 1996, p. 17.

31 Robert Power to Ron Yurick, letter, July 14, 1995.

32 Ron Yurick to Gordon McGuinty, letter, August 4, 1995.

33 G.F. Lee and A. Jones-Lee, "Practical Environmental Ethics: Is There an Obligation to Tell the Whole Truth?" unpublished paper, G. Fred Lee & Associates, El Macero, California, p. 6.

34 G.F. Lee and A. Jones-Lee, "Environmental Ethics: The Whole Truth," *Civil Engi-neering*, October 1995, p. 6.

35 Lee and Jones-Lee, "Practical Environmental Ethics," p. 6.

36 G. Fred Lee and Associates, "Overview Assessment of the Potential Public Health, Environmental and Groundwater Resources and Other Impacts at the Proposed Adams Mine Landfill," December 12, 1995.

37 "Adams Mine PLC Has Study Reports," *The Temiskaming Speaker*, November 22, 1995.

38 "Dumping on Kirkland Lake," *Now*, November 24, 1995.

39 John Barber, "Adams Mine Plan a Non-starter," reprinted in *Northern Daily News*, December 1, 1995.

40 "Why Metro Trashed Mine as Landfill," *The Toronto Star*, February 6, 1996.

41 "Mine Site Dump Plan Gets Huge Blow," *The Toronto Star*, December 20, 1995.

42 "Why Metro Trashed Mine as Landfill," *The Toronto Star*, February 6, 1996.

43 Ibid.

CHAPTER 3. DONE DEAL, 1996–1999

1 "How Safe? What Did BFI Find That Made It Walk on the Adams Mine?" *High-Grader Magazine*, Summer 2000.

2 McGuinty, *Trashed*, p. 169.

3 Ibid., p. 184.

4 Ibid., p. 187.

5 Ibid., p. 189.

6 "Metro Solution under Discussion," *Northern Daily News*, April 25, 1995.

7 McGuinty, *Trashed*, p. 165.

8 "The Powers That Be," *HighGrader Magazine*, March 1998.

9 "Golf Buddy Says Harris Did Him No Favours," *Now*, June 25, 1998.

10 McGuinty, *Trashed*, p. 205.

11 Ibid., p. 56.

12 "Done Deal," *HighGrader Magazine*, March 1998.

13 "Developer Expects to Satisfy Concerns," *Kirkland Lake Gazette*, January 16, 1998.

14 Mark Winfield and Paul Muldoon, "Democracy and Environmental Accountability in Ontario," The Environmental Agenda for Ontario Project, April 1999.

15 Rick Lindgren, Notes on Meeting with Hydrogeologist Paul Bowen over the Golder Documents on the Adams Mine, internal memo, March 6, 1998.

16 Rick Lindgren, memorandum to AMIC Steering Committee, March 6, 1998, p. 1.

17 Ibid.

18 "Panel Asked to Debunk Myths about Landfill," *Kirkland Lake Gazette*, March 27, 1998.

19 "Engineers Offer Assurances about Dump," *Kirkland Lake Gazette*, April 15, 1998.

20 Department of Civil Engineering, University of Colorado, "Tailings and Mine Waste '96," A.A. Balkema Publishing, 1996.

21 Anthony Story, in his master's thesis, "The Engineering of Controversy: Environmental Consultants and Public Participation in the Adams Mine Landfill Proposal," concludes that the hearing was "a pitched battle of credentials" and Notre, having spent a fortune on consultants, was in a better position to win the battle.

22 "MOE Confident Water Flows into Pit," *Northern Daily News*, April 15, 1998.

23 "Decision Surprises Opponents," *Northern Daily News*, June 20, 1998.

24 E. Zaltsberg to D. Staseff, "Report on Results of Drilling, Testing and Groundwater Flow Modelling of Drill holes 98-1 and DH 98-2 Adams Mine Landfill, Prepared by Golder Associates," memo, December 4, 1998.

25 "Battle Is Now Over: McGuinty," *Northern Daily News*, September 28, 1998.

CHAPTER 4. DROPPING THE GLOVES, MAY–AUGUST 2000

1   I wrote about the event at the time in "Toronto Pols Go Airborne to Dodge Northern Garbage Protest," *Straight Goods*, May 2000.

2   "Protesters Go Away, *Northern Daily News*, May 29, 2000.

3   Hugh Reynolds, "Toronto's Visit to Adams Mine: Open Letter to Mayor Lastman," *The Temiskaming Speaker*, June 7, 2000.

4   Full-page ad, *The Temiskaming Speaker*, June 7, 2000.

5   "Ontario Won't Pay for Dump Substitute," *The Globe and Mail*, June 22, 2000.

6   "Bidding War over Toronto Garbage," *The North Bay Nugget*, June 24, 2000.

7   McGuinty, *Trashed*, p. 280.

8   "ONTC Warns Group: Adams Mine Protesters Warned to Stay Clear of Tracks," *Northern Daily News*, July 19, 2000.

9   "Critics Accuse Harris of Trying to Steer Toronto's Waste North to Benefit Friend," *The Globe and Mail*, July 22, 2000.

10 Deputy Minister Cameron Clark to Bill Saundercook, letter, June 20, 2000.

11 "Opponents Draw Line in the Sand," *Northern Daily News*, July 31, 2000.

12 "First Nation Promising to Do 'Whatever It Takes,'" *Northern Daily News*, August 23, 2000.

13 *Le peuple invisible* is the title of Richard Desjardin's 2007 National Film Board documentary on the Algonquin people.

14 "First Nation Promising to Do 'Whatever It Takes,'" *Northern Daily News*, August 23, 2000.

15 "Lastman Speaks Out for Garbage Plan," *The Toronto Star*, August 2, 2000.

16 "Opponents Take Fight to IOC," *The Toronto Star*, August 3, 2000.

17 "Trash Opponents Attack Toronto's Reputation: City Called 'Toxic Criminals' by Northern Residents," *The Toronto Star*, August 4, 2000.

18 "Kirkland Lake a Stop Gap," *The Toronto Star*, August 5, 2000.

19 "Protesters Declare War on Toronto, *Northern Daily News*, July 25, 2000.

20 Adams Mine Coalition, "Adams Mine Battle Heads to Europe," press release, August 23, 2000.

21 "Dump Foes Take Aim at Games Bid," *The Toronto Star*, August 10, 2000.

22 Ibid.

23 Interview with Terry Graves, April 15, 2012.

CHAPTER 5. THE RISING OF THE MOON, SEPTEMBER–OCTOBER 2000

1 Ipperwash Inquiry transcript, www.attorneygeneral.jus.gov.on.ca/inquiries/ipperwash, November 28, 2005.

2 "The Adams Mine Song" would be recorded on the Grievous Angels 2003 release *Hanging Songs*.

3 "Garbage Plan Could Be Headed for the Trash Heap," *The Globe and Mail*, September 29, 2000.

4 "Trash Pact Details Hidden," *The Toronto Star*, October 2, 2000.

5 Dr. Larry Jensen to Mayor Mel Lastman, letter, August 2, 2000.

6 "Delay Garbage Vote," *The Toronto Star*, October 3, 2000.

7 "Frenzied Mayor Fights to Push Garbage Through," *The Toronto Star*, October 6, 2000.

8 Ibid.

9 "Garbage Plan Vote for Next Tuesday," *The Globe and Mail*, October 7, 2000.

10 "Police Poised to Dump Protesters," *The North Bay Nugget*, October 7, 2000.

11 "Opposition Escalates," *Northern Daily News*, October 4, 2000.

12 "Heating Up," *Northern Daily News*, October 5, 2000.

13 "Trash Plan Getting Rough Ride," *The Toronto Star*, October 5, 2000.

14 "Chaos, Confusion Mark the Great Trash Debate," *The Toronto Star*, October 11, 2000.

15 Global TV News, October 10, 2000.

16 *The Toronto Sun*, October 15, 2000.

17 "Lastman Sinks Political Capital into Garbage Pit," *The Globe and Mail*, October 11, 2000.

18 "Landfill Deal Faces Threat," *Northern Daily News*, October 13, 2000; conversation with Olivia Chow, January 31, 2013.

19 "Native Leader Vows Fight Bigger Than Oka," *The Toronto Star*, October 11, 2000.

20 City TV News, October 11, 2000.

21 "Adams Mine? That Project Is D-E-D," *National Post*, November 7, 2000.

22 Ibid.

23 Royson James, *The Toronto Star*, October 21, 2000.

24 "Opponents to Adams Mine United and Growing," *The Temiskaming Speaker*, October 18, 2000.

CHAPTER 6. BATTLE ON THE 401, 2001–2002

1   Gordon McGuinty to Rob Power, e-mail, January 4, 2001.

2   "Harris Pulls Out All the Stops to Save Adams Mine Garbage Plan," *Straight Goods*, February 26, 2001.

3   McGuinty to Power, e-mail, January 4, 2001.

4   Gordon McGuinty to John Weir, fax, re: City of Toronto Disposal Costs, January 9, 2001.

5   "Canada Down in the Dumps," *Maclean's*, February 26, 2001.

6   "Harris Said to Favour Mine Site Proposal," *The Toronto Star*, February 10, 2001.

7   "Tories Help Michigan in Garbage Appeal," *The Toronto Star*, February 9, 2001.

8   "Premier Working to Reopen Garbage Plan, Sarnia Mayor Says," *The Toronto Star*, February 10, 2001.

9   "Tories Help Michigan Garbage Site Appeal," *The Toronto Star*, February 9, 2001.

10 "Adams Link to U.S. Michigan Governor Gets Advice on Killing Dump Deal," *The Toronto Star*, March 7, 2001.

11 Ibid.

12 Ibid.

13 Don Wanagas and Mark Gollom, "Adams Mine Plan Could Be Revived by Province: Request for Briefing: London Mayor Objects to Garbage Being Routed through Her City," *National Post*, February 8, 2001.

14 McGuinty, *Trashed*, p. 328.

15 "Plan 9 from Kirkland Lake," *HighGrader Magazine*, September 2001.

16 "The Word That Turns Council Spines to Jelly," *The Toronto Sun*, September 9, 2001.

17 "Playing Hardball: Enouy Threatens to Withdraw Composting Proposal," *Northern Daily News*, November 21, 2001.

18 "The Word That Turns Toronto Council to Jelly," September 9, 2001.

19 McGuinty, *Trashed*, p. 335.

20 Ibid., p. 343.

21 Ibid., pp. 343–4.

CHAPTER 7. THE SACRIFICE ZONE, 1999–2002

1 "PCBS R Us," *HighGrader Magazine*, September 1999.

2 "U.S. Military's Dangerous Waste to Be Dumped in Canada," *Straight Goods*, January 28, 2000.

3 "The Generation and Management of Hazardous Wastes and Transboundary Waste Shipments Between Mexico, Canada and the United States Since NAFTA: A 2004 Update," The Pembina Institute, 2004.

4 "Dumping on the Desperate," *HighGrader Magazine*, January 2000.

5 "PCBS R Us," *HighGrader Magazine*, September 1999.

6 Ibid.

7 "Paying the PCB Piper," *HighGrader Magazine*, March 2000.

8 Ibid.

9 Ibid.

10 Basel Action Network, "No Dumping on Wake Island," press release, May 8, 2000.

11 "Launching Solutions to Our Toxic Legacy," *The Seattle Times*, April 12, 2000.

12 "What Part of No?" *HighGrader Magazine*, May 2000.

13 "Monsanto Hid Decades of Pollution," *The Washington Post*, January 1, 2002.

14 Neil Tangri, "Waste Incineration: A Dying Technology," Global Anti-Incineration Alliance, 2003.

15 John Bennett interview, *Wall Street Corporate Reporter*, December 20, 1999.

16 "Keep the Home Fires Burning," *HighGrader Magazine*, September 1999.

17 "Poisonville: America's Toxic Pipeline into the Heart of Northern Ontario," *HighGrader Magazine*, March 2002.

18 "Write Yer Own EA," *HighGrader Magazine*, Summer 2002.

19 Public Concern Timiskaming, "Bennett Bogged Down by Incinerator Battle," press release, May 6, 2002.

20 Brit Griffin, "Background Record of Bennett Environmental's Operating History from Sumas British Columbia to RSI, St. Ambroise, Quebec," prepared for the Temiskaming Federation of Agriculture, September 2, 2002.

21 Brit Griffin, "The Times Beach Connection," *HighGrader Magazine*, Spring 2002.

22 "State Firm on Rule for Incinerator: 99.9999% of Dioxin Must Be Destroyed," *St. Louis Post-Dispatch*, January 24, 1993.

23 "Keep the Home Fires Burning," *HighGrader Magazine*, September 1999.

24 Griffin, "Background Record of Bennett Environmental's Operating History . . . " September 2, 2002.

25 Ibid.

26 Brit Griffin, "Invasion of the Process Snatchers," *HighGrader Magazine*, Summer 2002.

27 Public Concern Timiskaming, "MOE Attempts to Squash Accident Reports on Incinerator," press statement, June 24, 2002.

28 "Fugitive Emissions," *HighGrader Magazine*, April 2000.

29 Dr. Riina Bray of the College to Ministry of Environment, letter, August 30, 2002.

30 *Wall Street Transcript*, December 3, 2001.

31 Public Concern Timiskaming, press release, May 9, 2002.

32 "Town Left in Pollution Hell," *The Irish Independent*, July 21, 2002.

33 Brit Griffin, "Scary Dairy: PCB Fears Freak Dairy Producers," *Now*, July 25, 2002.

34 Robert Poirier to David Ramsay, letter, June 7, 2002.

35 Julian Porter to Peter Nicoll, Beak Consulting, letter, August 22, 2002.

36 Temiskaming Federation of Agriculture, "Farmers Accuse Bennett of Withholding Toxic Burning Plans from EA," press release, August 2, 2002.

37 Alan D. Levy, "Scoping Issues and Imposing Time Limits by Ontario Environment Minister and Environmental Assessment Hearing," *Journal of Environmental Law and Practice*, Vol. 10, No. 2, May 2001.

38 "Write Yer Own EA," *HighGrader Magazine*, Summer 2002.

39 "The Dog Ate My Homework," *HighGrader Magazine*, Christmas 2002.

40 James O'Mara, Director, Environmental Approvals Branch, to Danny Ponn, letter, November 1, 2002.

CHAPTER 8. THE FINAL REEL, 2003–2011

1 Golder, "Preliminary Hydrogeological Investigation," December 1990, p. 39.

2 Dr. Ken Howard, "The Adams Mine Landfill Proposal: An Independent Review and Critical Analysis of Hydrogeological Investigations and Recent Monitoring Data," August 12, 2003.

3 "Stockwell Supports Adams Mine Plan," *The North Bay Nugget*, March 14, 2002.

4 McGuinty, *Trashed*, p. 348.

5 "Developer's Tory Ties Run Deep," *The Toronto Star*, May 9, 2003.

6   Ibid.

7   "Tory Dump Play," *HighGrader Magazine*, March 2003.

8   Ibid.

9   "Backroom Stinker," *Now*, March 2003

10 "CN's Motive Challenged," *The North Bay Nugget*, February 12, 2003.

11 Caverly later gave a sworn affidavit to Terry Graves outlining everything that had been said at the meeting.

12 A confidential source had provided details relating to the negotiations between the MNR and the 1532382 Ontario Inc.

13 Ken Seim (MNR) to Ivan Cragg (MNR), e-mail, February 23, 2003.

14 Owen Smith to Vic Prasad, Ministry of Natural Resources, letter, April 7, 2003.

15 Craig Greenwood to Owen Smith, letter, April 16, 2003.

16 MNR briefing note, October 6, 2003.

17 "Government Accused of Secret Land Deal," *The Globe and Mail*, May 8, 2003.

18 Statement of Defence, Notre Development Corporation/1532382 Ontario Inc. and Canadian Waste Services, Ontario Superior Court of Justice, April 17, 2003.

19 "Probe Ordered into Loans of Tory Backer," *Canadian Press*, June 3, 2003.

20 MNR memo, April 17, 2003.

21 "Video of Harris Raises Dump Fears," *The Toronto Star*, May 16, 2003.

22 "Stockwell Supports Adams Mine Plan," *The North Bay Nugget*, March 14, 2002.

23 "Leaks Make Adams Mine Unsafe as Dump Critics Say," *Canadian Press*, May 26, 2003.

24 "Adams Mine Presents Stink at Queen's Park," *The Temiskaming Speaker*, May 28, 2003.

25 "Stockwell Quits over Expenses," *National Post*, June 17, 2003.

26 Gordon McGuinty to John Burke, MNR, e-mail, July 23, 2003.

27 Ken Howard, "An Independent Review and Critical Analysis of Hydrogeological Investigations and Recent Monitoring Data," executive summary, August 12, 2003.

28 David Staseff, MOE memo, January 26, 2004.

29 E. Zaltsberg to D. Staseff, memo, December 4, 1998.

30 Brit Griffin, "The McGuinty Cousins and Adams Mine" *HighGrader Magazine*, Winter 2004.

31 Ibid.

32 Editorial, *Sault Star*, November 21, 2003.

33 "Thousands Object to Draining of Adams Mine," *Canadian Press*, January 4, 2004.

34 Adams Mine Coalition, "Northerners Call for Meeting with Minister over Adams Mine," press release, November 17, 2003.

35 Mark Puumala, Dr. Ken Howard, MOE internal notes, December 2003.

36 "Feud Flares Up," *Northern Daily News*, June 17, 2003.

37 *Hansard*, February 28, 2007.

38 In the Matter of an Arbitration under Chapter Eleven of NAFTA and the UNCITRAL Arbitration Rules between Vito Gallo and the Government of Canada, Award, September 15, 2011, p. 57.

CONCLUSION: STEPPING OUT OF THE BOX

1 McGuinty, *Trashed*, p. 143.

Index